Everytime
Press

IT'S ABOUT THE DOG

The A-to-Z Guide for Wannabe Dog Rescuers

GUILIE CASTILLO ORIARD

ISBN: 978-1-925536-19-5

Everytime Press
32 Meredith Street
Sefton Park SA 5083
Australia

Email: everytimepress@outlook.com
Website: https://www.everytimepress.com
Everytime Press catalogue:
https://www.everytimepress.com/everytime-press-catalogue/

Cover photographs copyright © Guilie Castillo Oriard
Author photograph copyright © Miguel Russo Hart
Cover design by Matt Potter

Also available as an eBook
ISBN: 978-1-925536-20-1

Everytime Press is a member of the
Bequem Publishing collective
http://www.bequempublishing.com/

For Sasha
(aka Tiny Dog)

You were loved. Yes, you were.

Contents

In the Beginning...

It's late on a Saturday night. Late enough that several of the guests who came for dinner have already left. By the light of the citronella candles that haven't yet sputtered out, we're polishing off the last bottle of wine with the three or four friends who don't have a babysitter waiting, clock in hand, back home. Conversation has ranged from politics to religion to gossip, and now turns to dogs. Three of our four are splayed around the table, and one, who fancies herself a gatekeeper, lies in wait by the door to the living room for an unsuspecting victim to trip.

Someone asks about her breed; I reply I have no idea. "Probably a mix of Corgi and—well, something. They're all from the street."

Everyone laughs. "Selikor terriers, eh?"

"Westpointers," someone else says.

This is Curaçao slang for local mutts, I learn. Westpunt, being the westernmost tip of the island, is considered "out in the sticks" for Willemstad dwellers. Selikor is the island's waste management company. (Prescient, and all too sad, in a community that treats unwanted pets as trash.)

"So where did you get them?"

"Just picked them up," I say. "One by one they showed up at the parking lot where I work, and no one wanted them, so—"

"So here we are." Cor, my partner, shrugs in mock resignation and everyone laughs again. He never wanted dogs, but these four furry packets of unconditional love have won him over. I've seen how he talks to them when he thinks no one is watching. How they seek him out unprompted for a bit of loving. How gentle his hands have become as he absent-mindedly strokes their ears or the underside of their necks.

"You should volunteer with CARF," one of our friends says. "They're always looking for help, and they're doing great work."

But I have no clue what he's talking about. At my blank look, his jaw drops. "You've never heard of CARF?"

And, just like that, my life changed forever.

~ * ~

This scene took place at the end of the summer of 2012. In the next five years, the dog population at our house would double (at times even triple) and—much more significantly—I would discover just how little about rescue I actually knew.

When people ask, I always take pride in saying I've been rescuing since I was a child. My mother loved animals, and our house in México always had a stray or two, ostensibly waiting to be placed at a good home although more often than not they ended up as permanent members of the family. Thus indoctrinated from earliest childhood (some might argue the womb), when I moved out to a place of my own I followed in these footsteps—hence the four furry packets of love in the house by the time of this late-night conversation in the summer of 2012. But it wasn't until after I began volunteering here in Curaçao—first with CARF, which I found out stood for Curaçao Animal Rights Foundation and was at the time the only rescue organization on the island; later with other animal welfare foundations that sprouted up to tackle, inasmuch as possible, the unmanageable stray- and abandoned-animal problem—that I came to the realization that, when it came to dog rescue and in spite of my early initiation, I was nothing but a hobbyist. At best. At worst, for as long as I'd been "rescuing" I'd actually been, recklessly and cluelessly, putting at risk the very lives I so wanted to save.

The lessons I've learned since that summer are many and varied (hence this book), but they all add up to one overarching principle, a sort of red thread that weaves them together into a fundamental paradigm. You see, my rescues had always been about me: about my conscience, about making myself feel better. How could *I* leave the dog out there? How could *I* sleep knowing he was hungry, or mistreated, or scared? *Me, me, me.*

It's not about me. Or you. It's not about assuaging our own morals, or paying tribute to our righteousness. No, it's about the *dog*. About improving *their* quality of life.

It's like paramedics. They're not working double shifts in the middle of the night *to feel better about themselves.* Or *to make friends.* When they pull you out of your mangled car after a crash, they don't go, "Aw, you poor thing... I'll take you home, fix you right up, and we'll live happily ever after," do they? No. And I bet social workers wish they could take home the kids they see living in bad conditions, but—never mind the law doesn't allow it—they understand their role is not that of a parent, or even a friend. Their job—some would say their *calling*—is to safeguard the child's rights, to make the tough decisions that protect his or her best interests. No room for the social worker's ego or righteousness or emotional needs, or even their emotional involvement—and how can they *not* become involved, right? Why? Because it's about the child.

Well, in rescue *it's about the dog.*

I'll close with a disclaimer: I'm no expert. The only thing that qualifies me to talk about dog rescue—and I use the word *qualify* rather loosely—is the fact that I've botched more than my share. And, possibly the fact that I care enough about that homeless dog in your neighborhood, the one that makes your heart shrink when you see him, to want to help you help him.

This book, therefore, is my attempt to collect the lessons I've learned—the most important ones, the key bits that have made the biggest difference to me as a rescuer. Some of them I learned early; most of them I learned much, much later. A lot of them

I'm still learning—and I hope to continue learning for the rest of my life. Maybe this is a journey you and I can share.

One More Thing...

Rescue isn't restricted to dogs; all sorts of different animals, domesticated or wild, are in need of human help, and—fortunately—there are many organizations devoted to providing it. Horses, farm animals, wolves, endangered species, laboratory rats... You name it, there's someone out there working overtime to help them live a life free of cruelty.

This book, however, is dog-centered. Blame the author for the discrimination. Dogs are the one animal I've rescued most often. Sure, there have been cats and birds and even the occasional reptile, but it's dogs that have taken up the larger part of my rescue endeavors. I'm much better at catching a dog than, say, a cat. I have only a notion of what an iguana eats, and I know the mere basics of the anatomy of a bird. (A couple of months ago a wild parrot, apparently hurt and unable to fly long distances, landed in our yard. Through caring for him over a couple of days, I learned more about parrots than I ever knew—including the fact that the best way to get a hold of them, assuming they don't know how to hop up on your finger or arm, is around the neck. No, it doesn't harm them—grabbing them from somewhere else, though, can and usually does. Who knew?)

Much about dog rescue, though, applies to any kind of rescue. If you're not so much into rescuing dogs as, say, opossums or rabbits or—why not—Komodo dragons, I'm hoping you'll find information here you can put to good use. (Well, maybe not for the Komodos. We don't really cover body armor in this book.)

I live in Curaçao, and, logically, that's where most of my rescue efforts happen. It's also where I've learned to be a rescuer (rather than a hobbyist) so many of my anecdotes and examples are Curaçao-centered. But I realize many of you, readers, will probably be from other places, and although perhaps 98% of the information in these pages is relevant no matter where you live (and rescue), I hope one of the most powerful takeaways here is consulting with local vets and local rescuers. That becomes doubly important if you're based somewhere else than Curaçao.

Introduction

There are so many misconceptions about dog rescue. Many people see it as a fad, a sub-theme of the veganism and sustainability tree-hugging movement. Or a sort of hobby: *Oh, you do rescue? That's cool. I do crochet.*

Or they confuse it with fostering, or with adoption. I hear it all the time: *We rescued our dog from the shelter.* No, guys. The dog was already safe at the shelter. You may have *adopted* a dog from the shelter (something for which all of us are eternally grateful to you)—but the dog was rescued by someone else.

The truth is that most people don't know what *rescuing* really is. Or what it takes. (Or what it gives.)

So, What Exactly is Rescue?

Picture this: You get a call. A dog's been sighted, they need extra hands. You drop what you're doing and jump into your car. You'll spend the next hour (or hours) in the sun, on hands and knees, running through brush, crossing busy intersections, in the effort to Catch This Dog. Eventually, once the dog is in a transport crate (and everyone is exhausted), you'll drive to the vet, get a pile of meds, then drive to the foster. Once the dog is settled there, you're done. You can go back to your day now.

That's rescue.

RESCUE
(from the street to safety)

|

to

|

FOSTERING
(healing)

|

to

|

ADOPTION
(a permanent home)

Rescue is the first of a three-step process through which a dog living in the streets (or in a bad home situation) regains quality of life. It involves locating, approaching, and catching a dog who, more often than not, will be fearful and wary of humans, and bringing him/her to a safe environment where s/he can regain health and trust in humans. Fostering is a huge part of the process, as is adoption—the ultimate happy ending—but they're *not* rescue.

The misconceptions extend to those involved in rescue, too. Some people think rescuers are a mix between superhero and saint. Others see us as dysfunctional hoarders, as bullies who stick our nose in everyone's business. Some as guileless fanatics with our hearts on our sleeves.

And it's not really surprising. Because rescuers rarely talk about it. After all, most of us prefer animals over people.

No, we were not born this way. Our "introversion"—*misanthropy* sounds so harsh—most often stems from the belief, backed up by what we see *every single day,* that most humans are hopelessly, irredeemably cruel—whether by ignorance or by intent.

And maybe that's true. But even if it is, it's still only *most* humans. Not *all.* And I want to be hopeful, rather than hopeless. I want to believe that there is redemption for the cruelty we, as a species, have wrought on the world. And I want to believe that, by sharing an insider's look at the actual how-to of rescuing, and doing it with more humor than cheesiness, and more practical advice than tear-jerker pleas, maybe some of these misconceptions might go the way of the dodo. Maybe someone with their heart in the right place might find out that rescuing isn't all that hard, something only saints and superheroes can do, and the next time they come across a dog in distress, they might actually be able to help—and help for real.

You see, dog rescue may not be thermonuclear mechanics, but things can go wrong very fast. As well-meaning as you might be, if you attempt a rescue without some knowledge of the basics you might actually do more harm than good. You might be taking a mom away from her newborn puppies (and sentencing those puppies to death). You might be interfering with a rescue effort already in motion (which will result in losing the dog, perhaps forever). You might hurt, or even kill, the dog you're trying to help. You might hurt yourself. You might get someone else hurt. You might bring any number of dangers, including disease, into your home.

This book, more than any manipulative plea for the welfare of animals, is rather intended as a guide—for that slice of the population that makes the difference between *most* and *all*—on How To Rescue A Dog. It's not about providing the motivation (there are millions of rescue videos and stories out there which will do that much more effectively); instead, it's about brief and practical guidelines. A blow-by-blow on the how-to. A glance at considerations (safety, medical, fostering). Bloopers. Humor. Some seriousness, too. (But not too much.) The Dog Rescuer's Kit, for instance, will list items every dog rescuer needs to carry. Under *H* you'll find a section about *Health Issues*; under *C* one on the nigh-impossible ones (*Catch Me If You Can*). And the O section is devoted to *Other Options*, a list of ideas for the people who can't rescue but still want to help.

I realize animal rescue is not a popular subject. Most animal lovers are more into breeding and dog shows than into tick-ridden, emaciated 10-year-old mutts abandoned and tied to a tree somewhere. Most people, in fact, would simply rather not know (let alone *do*).

But *most* is not *all*.

If this book has found its way into your hands, maybe you're one of those people who stands between *most* and *all*. Maybe you're looking to become a rescuer yourself. Maybe you've become unable to turn a blind eye when you see skinny and scared dogs wandering the streets. Maybe there's a specific dog you want to help. Or maybe you have friends who rescue, and you want to understand what the whole shindig is about. Maybe you like those rescue shows on TV, and you've been wondering if you could do it. Maybe you're just curious.

Whatever the reason, I hope the information in these pages not just quenches your curiosity but broadens your perspective—and, along the way, maybe gives you a giggle or two. And if you find yourself reaching for a tissue more than once, then I congratulate you. The kind of heart you have is a rare, rare thing—and the world needs more of you.

Chapter 1

Assessment

Every situation—every dog—is different; no two rescues are the same. That's why **assessment** is so very, very important before you jump in.

But assess *what*, exactly? And *how*?

It's about two things: *history*, which will tell you what kind of rescue it'll be, and *health*, to know how urgent the rescue is.

History

A dog ends up on the street in one of four ways:
- s/he got lost,
- s/he was abandoned,
- s/he ran away, or
- s/he was born there (what we call *feral*).

Signs that a dog is lost

Look for a collar, tag, recently brushed coat, cleanliness, clipped nails, few ticks or fleas (or none); any signs that a human somewhere cares. The dog will often look disoriented and distressed. Usually easy to approach. Might be neutered/spayed (easy to see in males; for females you'll need to look for a scar on their belly).

Signs that a dog is abandoned

Like lost dogs, abandoned ones will most likely look disoriented and distressed, and may also be easy to approach, but chances are they haven't been treated as nicely by human hands, so perhaps they won't be quite as trusting. They'll most likely lack

19

a collar and tag, although there may be a mark on the fur around their neck where a collar used to be. (If you abandon your dog, you'd probably take off any marks or items that would identify him/her as yours, right?) Indications of human care won't be as recent: coat beginning to look matted, chipped or torn nails, fleas and ticks might be prevalent, signs of recent weight loss: loose skin, head looks disproportionately large. If s/he has been on the street for a while, s/he will most likely be skeletal; home-raised dogs lack the street smarts to find food easily. Disease is one of the main reasons dogs are abandoned or neglected, so look for skin issues, growths or lumps.

Signs that a dog is a runaway

Indications of human care, if present at all, will not be recent: matted fur, torn nails, signs of abuse (wounds or scars). Look for an old collar or other signs of tethering, maybe a torn leash or a broken chain dragging behind him/her. Lots of ticks and fleas. The dog might look distressed, but not as disoriented as a lost or abandoned one. S/he will most likely be wary, if not outright defensive, when approached, even—maybe especially—when food is involved. S/he's been tricked before. S/he knows humans can be very, very cruel.

Signs that a dog is street-born (feral)

No indications of human care at all, and usually an obvious aversion to any human interaction. May be thin, even skinny, but will rarely be as emaciated as a lost or abandoned dog; a feral will have learned very early on how and where to procure food, how to defend it, how to survive. Lots of ticks and/or fleas. Usually visible skin conditions (bald, scaly, or scabbed patches, or near-total hair loss). Usually seem self-assured, like they know where they're going. Will probably show distress or wariness when approached. They'll back away, or growl, snap, or bark a warning. Probably won't be neutered/spayed.

Dogs who have 'misplaced' their homes, whether they escaped in pursuit of a female in heat and can't find their way back, or whether they were purposefully abandoned by their owners, are often the easiest rescues. They're used to humans being a source of security, so they'll be approachable—or might even approach you. They're used to being handled, so slipping a leash on them should be a piece of cake. They might be disoriented and panicked, though, so you do want to keep your wits about you. They might also be seriously hurt; home-raised dogs, being strangers to the street, are at high risk of getting hit by a car or attacked by other dogs. If they've been out on the street a while, they might be hungry enough to have eaten something harmful (like swallowing whole a hamburger wrapped in paper or plastic) and might need immediate veterinary intervention.

Dogs purposefully leave behind the safety of a home, with no intention of returning, for only one reason: survival. A runaway dog is one who's been abused to the point where his/her survival instinct kicked in and told him/her to flee. For obvious reasons, these dogs are often as distrusting of humans as a feral dog (if not more).

Ferals have a very different attitude to humans than those who've had (good) families. They're survivors, they're strong and smart. Smart enough to know not to trust humans. For a street-born, humans are another danger to avoid, like fast-moving cars or fireworks. They've seen a lot more abuse, so they'll be wary if not outright scared. (A fearful dog does *not* an easy rescue make.)

Health

Assessing a dog's history will help you plan the *how* of your rescue: will you need traps and drugs, will you need days of trust-building, or will the dog jump into your car at the first opportunity? But it's their health that will determine the urgency of the rescue. Even without a veterinary degree, you can still look for some tell-tale signs of possible life-threatening conditions that will help you get your priorities in order.

- How malnourished is the dog? (Can you see ribs? Can you count them?)
- Does s/he have visible skin issues?
- Watery eyes and/or nose? Nervous "tics", trouble walking? (These may be signs of canine distemper.)
- Does s/he eat well? Any vomit and/or diarrhea? (These may indicate parvovirus, intestinal infections, and/or parasites.)
- Is the dog visibly disabled or hurt? (Look for limping, open wounds, impaired vision or hearing, etc.)
- If the dog is female, do her teats look elongated and swollen? (She might be suckling, and you'll want to rescue the puppies, too.)
- Also for females, remember to check for an enlarged vulva; if she's in heat, rescue urgency increases.
- IMPORTANT: In Curaçao we—fortunately—don't have the rabies virus (and, for the purposes of this book, I'm leaving rabies out of the equation), but if you live, and plan to rescue, in an area where rabies might be a risk, please know that catching a dog with rabies is best left to the professionals. If a dog has difficulty swallowing, makes choking sounds, is foaming at the mouth, exhibits fear of water, is having seizures or trembling uncontrollably, you might have a rabid animal on your hands. Well, no, *not* on your hands, please. This is when you call in the big guns. (And please do call them. Death by rabies is not just a public hazard but also a harrowing way for any creature to die.)

You'll find a more extensive description of conditions and diseases often present in rescue dogs in Chapter 9, *Health Issues* (p. 63). None of this, however, is meant to give you any authority to treat the dog, but only to help you decide the when and the how of your rescue. Treatment, and all health-related judgment calls, must always remain the exclusive prerogative of a veterinarian.

Chapter 2
Body Language

If you are a dog lover, you've probably wished more than once that dogs could speak. If they could tell us where it hurts, what they like, ask us questions like *when will you be back*—and understand the answer.

Verbal communication has become indispensable to us humans, but our reliance on it has more to do with our being lazy rather than on any intrinsic efficacy of the spoken word. Because, when it comes down to it, *what* is said is less important than *how* it's said. And not just the tone or volume, mind you; it's also about the *attitude* of the person speaking. Imagine you're watching a conversation among strangers, one you can't actually listen to; maybe they're too far away, maybe they're behind a window. Without hearing the words, without even trying to lip-read, you can tell a lot about what's happening: whether it's an argument or a friendly chat, whether a story is being told or whether opinions are being exchanged. You can tell whether the people involved are in agreement or at odds. You can sense hostility or love, enthusiasm or boredom.

It should come as no surprise, then, that dogs do, in fact, communicate. Not verbally, no, but in spite of this—or maybe because of it—they do so much more effectively than humans do. The language of dogs (yes, it *is* language) relies "on phonemes made from rumps, heads, ears, legs, and tails."[1] Being a language of the body, it leaves no room for misunderstandings, no potential for lies or secrets.

---

[1] Alexandra Horowitz, *Inside of a Dog: What Dogs See, Smell, and Know*, Scribner 2009

Once we humans understand it, that is. And that, right there, is your challenge. If you're going to start approaching strange dogs on the street, you'll need to gain at least a grasp on the basics of Dogspeak. This is a quick-and-dirty cheat sheet to start you out, and maybe to serve as a checklist to have on hand, but there are many broader resources out there—YouTube videos, blogs, trainers, books (my favorite is *Canine Body Language: A Photographic Guide*, by Brenda Aloff, Dogwise Publishing, 2005)—and, if you're serious about becoming involved in dog rescuing, I highly recommend you get your hands on a few.

Contrary to what many people believe, a dog bites only as a last recourse to protect him/herself. Prior to the bite, s/he gave you all sorts of signals and warnings. S/he *communicated* his/her discomfort and anxiety. And *you* didn't listen. So here is a guide to a dog's most common stress signals—and a few friendly "words" you can learn in order to start the conversation off on the right foot.

Stressed Behavior

Stress in dogs is a sign of discomfort, anxiety, nervousness, apprehension, or uncertainty. Whatever you're doing is making the dog uncomfortable. You're invading his/her space, s/he can smell the adrenaline on you (dogs interpret that as unpredictability, which makes them wary), you're looking them in the eye (eye contact, especially when sustained, represents a threat in the animal world), you're crouching above them (which is interpreted as domineering), you're approaching too fast... Any of the above, and—because dogs are individuals—so many more, may produce stress. You can recognize it by these signals listed on the next two pages:

Signs a dog is stressed
- avoidance (moving away, looking away)
- lip lick
- yawning
- paw lift
- panting
- whale eyes (when you can see the white of the eyes)
- toes spread
- sniffing (where there's nothing to sniff)

Signs a dog is anxious
- hyper vigilant
- sniffing (where there's nothing to sniff)
- tail low
- cautious
- fidgeting
- fast movements
- signs that s/he's trying to get away

Signs a dog is fearful (submissive)
- tail low, or—in extreme fear—tucked between the legs
- head low
- body sinking to the ground
- avoiding eye contact
- trying to make themselves look smaller, disappear
- low warning barks
- ears flattened
- low wagging tail

Signs a dog is fearful (aggressive)
- stand taller (make themselves look bigger, to scare you away)
- stiff body posture
- ears pricked up
- legs spread

- warning barks (usually pitched low)
- full-on eye contact (threat)
- bared teeth
- snapping

Dogspeak 101

If you've ever observed two dogs meeting for the first time, you've probably seen—or at least sensed—a conversation happening. These two dogs will tell each other, quite clearly, what's acceptable and what's not. They'll make invitations to play, they'll ask for permission to approach or to sniff each other, they'll accept (or refuse) closer interaction. Unless you're an experienced dog person, chances are that, although you may understand what's happening, you don't have much of a grasp as to the *how*.

The good news? Dogspeak is a simple language compared to some of the garbles we humans have managed to come up with (say, for instance, Dutch). Below I've listed a few bits, or 'phonemes', of dog language that behaviorists call *calming* or *negotiation signals*, and which you can use to establish trust with a fearful or skittish dog. Many of them, in fact, are included in the stress signals listed above; in interactions with humans, dogs use them to calm *us*. They're asking us, as politely as they can, to please not attack them.

Think of these as the ABCs of Dogspeak. Ready?

- **Lick your lips.** Slowly, so that the dog catches the movement; our tongues—our whole mouths, actually—are a lot less obvious than theirs.
- **Look away.** Even if just for a second or two. When the dog sees you actively break eye contact, s/he 'hears' you say, loud and clear, *I'm not a threat.*

- **Yawn.** If you've ever been in a highly stressful situation, or witnessed someone in one, you might have noticed some seemingly uncalled-for yawning. That's because yawning releases stress. *And* it's also highly contagious. Dogs know this, and use it to great advantage with each other. When you yawn, what a dog will 'hear' is, *"I don't want to be tense. Let's not be tense, okay?"*
- **Move slowly.** Speed is synonymous with aggression and threat.
- **Make your eyes soft.** Relax your face muscles, blink slowly.

Although the repertoire is much broader for dogs than it can be for humans (lifting a human 'paw', unfortunately, will most likely be associated with kicking for a street dog), there are a few that we can—and do—use to huge advantage. Using calming signals to converse with a stressed dog helps us communicate *I'm trying to make you comfortable.*

Chapter 3

Botched!

You know how they say *the road to hell is paved with good intentions*? Well, the person who said it first was a dog rescuer.

Okay, I don't actually know that. But it must've been. And I'm also pretty sure it was a dog rescuer who came up with *carpe diem*—although, honestly, in rescue it's more about seizing the *moment* rather than the day.

Good intentions are what bring you to the threshold of dog rescuing. But, once you cross over (*into the dark side, mwahahahahaha*), they'll be about as useful as... I don't know. A royal title.

The bad news is it's incredibly easy to botch a dog rescue. Nine times out of ten, though, it's your fault. And that's the good news. It means it's up to you *not* to botch it.

Botched #1: The Dog Ran Away

What You Did Wrong

You moved too fast. Good luck getting close to that dog again.

Do It Right

The goal is to get the dog to come to you—or, at the very least, to *give you permission* to come to them. If the dog backs away, stop. Don't invade their personal space until they're ready to allow you to.

Or Maybe...

You were nervous. Or tense. Or just excited. Animals can smell your adrenaline a mile away—and, to them, it smells of aggression.

Do It Right

Stay calm. Breathe. Get in touch with your Zen. *Don't approach until you're in your happy place.*

Botched #2: The Dog Growled or Snapped at You

What You Did Wrong

You invaded his/her space.

Do It Right

See Botched #1

Or Maybe...

You looked him/her right in the eye.

Do It Right

For dogs,[2] eye contact is confrontational. Aggressive. Avoid it like the plague. Keep it brief, and make a point of looking away while they're watching you. That's a "negotiation" signal, a way of saying, "I'm harmless." (Remember the ABCs of Dogspeak in Chapter 2, p. 27.)

Or Maybe...

You tried to touch him/her too fast.

Do It Right

If you're within a meter or two, offer your hand to be sniffed. Keep it below their nose level. Stretch out (*slowly*) your arm, palm up and fingers curled into a loose fist (best way to avoid losing a fingertip).

---

[2] Although humans bond through eye contact—we hold someone's gaze during conversation, we look into the eyes of those we meet as we shake hands, we even speak of the eyes as being a mirror of the soul—we do have some similarities with dogs in that eye contact can be confrontational. Try walking around town one day and meeting (and holding) the gaze of every single person you come across. Experiments have shown that we're not as comfortable with that as we think we are.

Botched #3: The Dog *Bit* You! Out of Nowhere!

(It wasn't *out of nowhere*. I hate to pop your bubble, honey, but you did it to yourself.)

What You Did Wrong

You tried to touch him/her too fast.

Do It Right

See Botched #2

Or Maybe...

You tried to pet the top of his/her head.

Do It Right

Your first touch should never—I repeat: *never*—be on the top of a dog's head. In Dogspeak, especially for dogs with reason to distrust humans, a hand above their heads feels threatening. Safe and friend-making areas to touch are the side of the neck, the underside of the chin, the chest, or the side of their bodies. As you gain acceptance, move to the area around the ears; they love that.

Botched #4: The Dog, Until then Docile and Friendly, Turned Psycho Killer When the Leash Came Out

What You Did Wrong

You presented the leash too fast.

Do It Right

Don't move on to the leash until the dog seems comfortable with you touching him/her. Present it for sniffing (like your hand, everything you present to the dog should be *below* nose level). Don't rush. Take your time—and let the dog take his/her time, too. If the dog seems okay with the leash (doesn't back away), keep going. Slip it around the neck as you continue petting them. Once the leash is in place, and while you're still petting them, begin to stand. Slowly. Read the dog. Make sure they're comfortable with everything you're doing.

Botched #5: You Got the Mama Dog, You Came Back for the Puppies— but They're Gone!

Well. Good luck finding them without the mom. If they're under 8 weeks, their instinct will tell them to hide. You won't get a peep from them. If they're older, they'll probably wander off when they get hungry. Best-case scenario, they'll be picked up by some kid who thinks they're "cute". More likely, though, and because there's no mom around to show them the ropes, they'll wander into traffic or fall into a drainage pipe or—. Ok. You get the picture. *Bad rescuer. Bad, bad.*

Do It Right

Don't get the mama dog until you've located the puppies. If you see a lactating female and no puppies in sight, you'll need to follow and/or observe until you can pinpoint where her litter is hiding. The good news is that once you have the puppies, especially if they're under 8 weeks, Mama won't bolt that fast, which might make it easier to get her, too.

Botched #6: You Interfered with an Ongoing Rescue Attempt

Remember what we said about good intentions? A well-meaning but clueless amateur can undo a rescue organization's work of *months* in... yeah, pretty quick.

Do It Right

Watch for signs this dog is being taken care of (see *Assessment*, p. 19), and if s/he looks like s/he hangs out at a regular place, you can ask locals if they know whether someone has been feeding, or otherwise looking after, that dog. The easiest (and surest) way, though, is to be in regular contact with your local rescue or shelter. Nowadays, with social media, it's so easy to snap a pic and post it to Facebook or Twitter and get an instant response.

~ * ~

Sometimes, though, all of the aforementioned is a luxury you won't be able to afford. If a dog is in an immediate life-threatening situation, you won't have time to wait, to choose your moment, to make friends, to call anyone, even to snap a picture. Saving the dog's life trumps everything.

But what if it's a rabid hundred-pound Mastiff with a lust for human flesh? (And, because Murphy's Law really *is* a law, you just know it'll be a dog like this that needs the most urgent help.) The next chapter, *Catch Me If You Can,* is a crash course on impossible rescues.

Chapter 4
Catch Me If You Can

Mark Twain wrote, "No good deed goes unpunished." We must prepare for the bruises and wounds that come with helping the helpless.
~ Roland D. Yeomans,[3] April 2016

Not every rescue is a *via crucis*. Sometimes rescue just... flows. Sometimes the stars seem to align for the rescuer—and for the dog. Sometimes the dog treats you like a long-lost best friend (and, who knows, maybe in another life you did know each other) and isn't just willing but eager to jump into your car. Sometimes all it takes is a couple of treats and a leash. I've seen rescues where the dog seemed to be waiting for the rescuers. In one case, they found out at the vet's that she was very sick. So sick, in fact, that she wouldn't have lasted another week, maybe not even another day, without immediate intervention. Did the dog put aside her fear of people because she knew, somehow, that she needed human help? Did her rescuer just do everything right? All we'll ever know for sure is that they both got lucky. (Yes, the dog did make it, and found a loving forever home.)

More often than not, though, rescue gets rough. And, because the universe loves irony, it's usually the dogs in most urgent need of help who refuse to cooperate. Because they're in panic, because they've been abused and don't trust humans, because they're hurt and in pain. Whatever the reason, it comes down to this:

---

[3] Roland, fellow writer, blogs at http://rolandyeomans.blogspot.com/

How do you catch a dog that doesn't want to be caught?

Chase & Corner

Put on your running shoes and your Einstein cap. If your friendliest, most patient attempts to approach the dog have failed, or if you're dealing with an emergency situation, you're going to have to do not just some sprinting but some fast, fast thinking. Get the dog to a place away from traffic, or other dangers, where you can corner him: alley, fenced yard, warehouse, anywhere that has only one way in or out—and, preferably, a narrow one you can block with your body.

Besides the running shoes, you'll need a leash—ideally a noose type (more on those in *The Dog Rescuer's Kit*, p. 85—and a couple of towels. If you're planning on using a transport crate, you may want to bring it into the area you've chosen for your chase showdown before you start the chase itself. But don't even try to chase the dog into it; they're smart, and a closed-off crate will be the last place they flee into. There's a reason traps are made of mesh (more on those at the end of this chapter).

In September 2012 a friend asked me to help him catch a dog who was hanging out in an empty lot behind one of those huge warehouse-type mega stores. "She's a little dog," he said, "but no one's been able to catch her." Even experienced rescuers had tried and failed. The people at a restaurant close by who had been feeding her (and who wanted to give her a home) couldn't get any closer to her than maybe three or four feet.

She was a tiny Maltese-like white dog, so small she was hard to spot among the grass and brush. Finally we did spot her, under the bed of an abandoned trailer, but as soon as we approached, she bolted. I knelt a few feet away, threw a few pieces of *leverworst* in her direction, and managed to lure her back: close enough to get a good look at her. She didn't look skinny, which was a good sign (and kudos to the restaurant people), but that meant, of course, that she had no real incentive to lower her guard and come closer.

We tried for days. Every morning I went back, sat in the dirt and in the sun, and threw pieces of leverworst cut in tiny cubes to keep her interested longer. On the second day she stopped running away and began waiting, never closer than her three-foot threshold, for me to throw the next goodie. On the third day she (finally!) took a piece from my outstretched fingers. But that was it. She refused to let me touch her, and—with surprising speed for such a small dog—she hurtled away as soon as I even *thought* about moving nearer to her.

And my friend was getting impatient. "We have no idea how old she is," he said. "Maybe she's pregnant. Maybe she's about to go into heat." She'd have a pack of dogs after her. She was so tiny she could easily be killed in the fray. Or by traffic. Or by any number of dangers. She was too small to survive in the street. It was a miracle she'd survived for however long she'd been out there.

Time for Plan B, then: Chase & Corner. Except there are no corners in a field. Aside from the mega store's outer wall, the terrain was all open. There were, however, some large trash bins that belonged to the restaurant, and by moving them against the wall we created a corner. My friend and I, each of us holding a big beach towel extended in front of us like a shield, would provide the two missing sides of the square and complete the illusion of a closed-off space. This illusion might just be enough to convince Tiny Dog to give up her wily Houdini ways.

And it worked—at first. We had built up enough trust with her that she barely hesitated before following the leverworst pieces I threw to the area between trash bins and wall. When we made our move with the towels and closed off her avenues of escape, she panicked only for a moment, and then sank into the grass to wait for the inevitable. We had her!

But cornering the dog is only 10% of the battle. Once s/he realizes there's no way out *except through you*, one of three things will happen—and you need to be prepared for all three. Or even for a mix of the three.

1. S/he'll submit

This is the best-possible scenario, the one you're hoping for—because it'll make everyone's life so much easier. But ask any rescuer: it's hard to see. A dog's surrender, especially that of a street-born dog who's been self-reliant all his/her life, is one of the toughest things to witness. They have no way of knowing you're their lifeline; at that point, you're the bad guy, the monster in the closet who came out and is now licking its chops. And still they give up. When Tiny Dog huddled down into the grass and looked up at us, as if pleading for mercy, my heart broke for her.

2. S/he'll make a run for it

A millisecond before my towel wrapped around Tiny Dog, she dashed between my legs and under the trash bins. My friend pounced, but it was too late: all we saw was a streak of white as she disappeared into the brush.

We had underestimated her. Misjudged her will and her resilience—and, most importantly, her fear. To be clear, a list of our mistakes:

- We trusted the trash bins as a reliable barrier. They weren't flush with the ground; they had wheels (that's how we moved them), and although the space under them looked too small for Tiny Dog to escape, we totally misjudged what desperation would make her capable of.
- We trusted ourselves (and our ridiculous towels) as reliable barriers. To a dog afraid of humans, a competent person may indeed represent the most unbreachable of barriers—key word being competent. We, on the other hand, behaved like

amateurs. We bought Tiny Dog's submission. We assumed, because of her size, she had no more fight in her. We should have seen her getaway run coming—and we should've been prepared to truncate it.

- We weren't ready with a leash. The most effective way to keep a dog from bolting once s/he's been cornered is with a leash around his/her neck. We did have leashes, but instead of having them primed—wide lasso loop, easy-slide knot—we had them draped across our chests. When Tiny Dog did her I give up routine, that was the perfect moment to slip a leash around her. One single move, one tug, leash snug around the neck... Then we really would have had her.

But even then it wouldn't have been quite over. There's a third option, remember?

3. S/he'll fight back

Once the possibility of escape is gone, especially once the leash goes around their neck, dogs who are unwilling to submit have only one option left: fight. They'll thrash and twist and flail, and empty their bowels and howl and scream. (If you've never heard a dog scream, brace yourself. It's enough to give you nightmares.)

Yes, it's horrible to listen to. And watch. But here's the thing: *you can't let go.* If you do, you're back to square one. No, actually you're worse off; you'll be at square *minus ten*, and it will take an enormous amount of convincing for that dog to even consider letting you near again.

The thrashing and screaming and pissing isn't the worst part, though. They'll also bite at anything within reach, including you.

Let's get our priorities straight. The goal here—the only one that counts, the one that trumps everything else—is Getting The Dog. Everything else (getting bitten, getting hurt, looking stupid, whatever) is important only in the measure that it affects Getting The Dog.

I know someone who was dragged sixteen feet over sharp rocks by a feral dog she'd been after for weeks and had just managed to leash. She could've let go, and she'd have ended up with maybe a scratch or two—but no dog. Instead, she delivered the dog to the foster (whom I was visiting) with blood trickling down both her shins. Her cuts looked deep enough for stitches. She was limping a bit, but she waved away the first-aid kit. "I got her," she said, with eyes shining.

Priorities.

While we're at it, let's get something else out of the way. There is no such thing as a vicious dog. What people see as "aggression" is, especially within the rescue context, fear. A dog will attack as a last resort only, and then only because s/he honestly believes his/her survival depends on it. When you don't have time to engage in Dogspeak conversation about how all this is for their own good, you need to be prepared to give some blood.

Come on. It's for a good cause.

The other thing they'll bite, in their thrash-and-pee mode, is the leash. I lost a dog that way once. Had her finally on a leash (after she bit me), and while we were waiting for someone to get the transport crate from the car—not even a minute—she bit her way through the leash and we had to start all over again.

Note to self: invest in a more resilient round-knit noose leash instead of the generic flat types you probably have lying around at home.

We, of course, never got that far with Tiny Dog. We made too many mistakes. Do not trivialize the Chase & Corner: it's an all-or-nothing approach. Now that all the trust we'd built was gone (square *minus ten*, remember?), we had no choice except move on to Plan C.

Which involved a trap.

Traps

If you're thinking of the bear kind, please forget those. Dog traps are basically long rectangles, usually made of small (but sturdy) mesh, and with a trigger door on one end. They do need to be rather large, at least three times the length of their intended occupant in order to be most effective. A street dog is smart, and a smart dog will be wariest of small, enclosed spaces.

They also need to be primed well. That doesn't mean just hardware, although it really is essential to keep the spring mechanism well oiled—the last thing you want is for the door to trigger shut before the dog is all the way in, or (maybe worse) to not trigger shut at all. But the bait is crucial. The trick is to use something irresistible (see *Food!*, p. 52)—which was a challenge in the case of Tiny Dog, since the restaurant people were feeding her all sorts of goodies: chicken, roast beef, sirloin, you name it. She was so well fed, in fact, that she picked out any stray vegetables that had made their way onto her plate and refused to eat them. Carrots, peas, even rice—*yuk yuk, ewwww*.

We asked the restaurant to please not feed her for 24 hours, in the hopes that, when faced with the scary-cage/yummy-smell-within choice, she'd be hungry enough to blow caution to the winds. The next morning my friend showed up with a trap he'd borrowed somewhere and with a chicken liver stew he'd spent the evening cooking. It smelled to high heaven, even with the lid still on, and as soon as we set down a few pieces around the trap, Tiny Dog peeked out of her hiding place.

We crumbled two or three chicken liver pieces and made a trail leading into the cage, and placed the full container (aka *mother lode*) right up against the trap's back end, so that in order to get to it she'd have to put all her weight, meager as it was, onto the platform that activates the door spring.

And then we waited. She grabbed the liver pieces furthest away, but seemed wary of coming any closer. We retreated to the car, about sixty feet away, and asked the restaurant people, who'd become eager spectators, to go back inside, too, and give her some space.

Traps do require patience. And, because they usually come into play with skittish dogs, micromanaging will work against you. You need to be prepared to walk away and come back later to check progress. Ideally, you'll find the door closed and the dog inside. Perhaps you'll find the trap empty, but the bait gone; then you'll need to check the spring mechanism, maybe do a test run.

But if you find the bait untouched—and you were using good stuff, such as, say, chicken livers—you have a problem. For any number of reasons, hunger didn't trump fear. Some of these reasons you can control: come back tomorrow with tastier bait, for instance. But chances are the dog won't risk the scary, evil-smelling cage even for raw steak if s/he has a reliable source of food somewhere else. Or if his/her level of fear is such that s/he'd rather starve than risk getting caught by humans.

Tiny Dog met both of these: she wasn't hungry (and probably hadn't been for a while; the restaurant people had been feeding her since they first spotted her in the empty lot a couple of weeks before), and she was very, very afraid of humans. (And our little stunt with the trash bins and towels did nothing to help.)

She ate all the liver pieces we'd strewn around the trap. She nibbled at the ones at the entrance to the trap, and stretched out her little body as much as she could to reach the ones farther inside—but at no point, and under no circumstance, did she put a single paw inside the trap. Not even on the edge.

And the clock was ticking. There was only one option left, but it was a nasty one.

Drugs.

Chapter 5

Drugs

I know what you're thinking. Why not skip all this *Catch Me If You Can* brouhaha—the chases and the panic, the risk of injury, the investment of time to build trust, the potential to ruin it all in one instant of faulty judgment—and just, you know, drug the dog?

Rescuers hate using drugs. Yes, because it feels like admitting defeat, but—more relevantly—because they can end in tragedy. Why?

- **It's a guess-timate.** The efficacy of tranquilizers is based on the animal's weight. In rescue, they're most frequently used when we can't get close enough to grab the dog—and if we haven't been close enough to grab 'em, we haven't been close enough to weigh 'em (or even judge their weight to a sufficient degree of accuracy). Give them too little and it won't work; but rounding your weight estimate up comes with its own perils.
- **Risk of overdose.** Give them too much and you could kill them. At the very least, you could do serious harm. The dog could have all sorts of medical conditions—heartworm, for instance, or anything that reduces their lung or cardiovascular capabilities, or liver disease—that can end in cardiac or respiratory arrest when the drug kicks in.
- **Risk of losing the dog.** The dog won't conveniently pass out within your sight. When a dog begins to feel the effects of the tranquilizer, they'll look for a safe place (i.e. away from

humans) to crash. You need to be prepared to follow (at a non-threatening distance) to avoid losing them.

- **You're only postponing the inevitable.** Drugs may seem like the easy way out, but they're not. If your reasoning for using drugs is based on the dog's 'aggression', think again. Tranquilizers won't turn this Cujo into Lassie. You'll still have to deal with a mouthful of teeth—and an intensified motivation to use them—when s/he wakes up.

Given all the above, you can understand why we weren't so gung-ho about using tranquilizers with Tiny Dog. But we were fresh out of options, and she was running out of time. She could go into heat at any moment, and when she did we'd lose her forever—best-case scenario. Worst-case, we'd find her dead somewhere, maybe run over by a car as she tried to escape the pack hounding her, or even killed by one of the dogs. (Yes, it happens.)

We needed to get her off the street.

Now that we'd moved on to the drug chapter of our rescue, only one decision remained: how to give her the tranquilizers. They can be administered in one of two ways:

Dart Guns

<u>Pros</u>: Great choice for ferals who shy away from even the most distant human contact. Because the drug goes in intramuscularly, and gets into the bloodstream faster, this is a fast-working tranquilizer.

<u>Cons</u>: You need a dart gun. And darts. With the right dose. And you need to be a very, very good shot. If you hit anything but pure muscle—an artery, say, or the spinal column, even the wrong nerve—you can maim, paralyze, or even kill the dog. Also, the sound of the shot will scare the dog away, which means it's—literally—a one-shot deal. S/he won't be eager to get within twenty meters of you ever again.

Oral Medication (pills, paste, powder, etc)

Pros: You don't need any special equipment. No chance of accidentally nicking an artery or nerve. No need to scare the dog with the gunshot sound: inserting pills in a chunk of liverwurst or sausage, or mixing paste or powder into a gravy-laden plate of food increases the chances they'll be consumed.

Cons: Unless you hand-feed them to the dog—and, honestly, if you can hand-feed the dog, why are you using drugs?—they can end up eaten by the wrong animal. Strays don't live in a vacuum; there are usually more dogs in the vicinity, which means that if you leave them for your intended 'victim' to find, another dog (or cat, or even bird) might find them first. They also take longer to work than darts, which gives the dog more time to get away from you. Pills need to be absorbed by the digestive system, so they'll work best on an empty stomach; you'll need to make sure the dog hasn't eaten, at least not substantially, before giving him/her the pills.

We didn't own a dart gun, didn't know anyone who did—and, even if we had, since we'd never fired one (or any other kind of gun), it wasn't really an option. That left tranquilizer pills, the kind so popular here in Curaçao at year's end, to help dogs deal with fireworks. Except they come in 5-kg brackets: 1-5 kg, 6-10 kg, 11-15 kg, so on. Which meant we needed to make a choice: was Tiny Dog under 10 kg, or over?

From the car, we watched Tiny Dog get her dinner from the restaurant people. She waited at a safe distance while the woman rinsed out her plate and filled it with what looked like strips of chicken, maybe turkey, in some sort of gravy. My mouth watered, but Tiny Dog took her sweet time. She waited until the door closed, then sniffed at the air for a good minute before taking the first step forward.

"How much do you think she weighs?"

"About... Eight kilos?"

Eight? I'd never owned, or even handled, a dog that came in at less than 13 kg.

"You think—less?"

"Maybe. No. I don't know. Small dogs aren't my thing. And she's so hairy."

We decided to go for the 6-10 kg pills. For one, I couldn't imagine any dog weighing less than 10 kg (barring really, really young puppies). And because she was so well-fed (and we couldn't guarantee no one would feed her for at least 12 hours before we gave her the pills), we were afraid the pills would at best make her only drowsy. Adrenaline is a great antidote to tranquilizers, so we needed her to pass out before we even approached.

I spoke to the restaurant people and explained our plan, asked them to please—please, *please*—not feed her the following day. They looked at me as if I were suggesting medieval torture, so we compromised: they'd give her half of her usual breakfast portion, and do it early in the morning. We'd give her the pills the following morning.

On D Day, my friend volunteered to be at Tiny Dog's lot at 6 am, in an attempt to ensure the pills—and the chunks of sausage we'd inserted them into—were the first thing she ate. The vet had told us the pills would take about an hour to kick in, but to wait a full two hours to ensure she'd be in a deep sleep before we approached her. My friend's job, then, wasn't just bringing the pills and sausage: he had to monitor that she did eat them, and had to keep an eye on where she chose to hide out when she started feeling wobbly. I would meet him there at 8 am to help with grabbing her and to take her to the vet.

At 7 am, though, he called me. "She's gone."

What? "Crap. Well, any idea where to look for her? I mean, did you see where—?"

"No, I meant she's gone as in... she's out. Like passed out. I've got her in my lap."

We met at the vet's, where we found out she had fleas and ticks, as well as tick fever (*ehrlichiosis*; see *Health Issues* on p. 64 for more detail). She was also a bit anemic (no surprise, given her pickiness with eating), but—great news: she did *not* have heart worms. She got antibiotics to treat the bacterial infection, deworming pills to take care of the intestinal parasites fleas transmit, and a follow-up appointment in two weeks to check on the anemia.

Tiny Dog slept through the entire examination, through the bath I gave her at home, and through most of the afternoon. At the vet's she'd weighed in at just over 4 kg. Gross miscalculation on our part, which earned us a scolding from the vet, and which didn't end in tragedy due to blind, stupid luck. Tiny Dog was young (the vet estimated around twelve months) and had, in spite of her health issues, a metabolism strong enough to process the drugs without going into respiratory or cardiac arrest. But that just goes to show how easy it is to miscalculate. If you're ever in a position to use tranquilizers for a rescue, remember this: long-haired breeds will tend to look heftier than short-haired ones, and larger breeds, even when emaciated, will probably weigh more than you think.

And always, always consult with a vet *beforehand*. No medication, no matter how "natural" or "organic" or "safe" it's labeled to be, should be administered to any animal without vet approval.

Seriously.

Ever.

P.S. — Tiny Dog's rescue story didn't end here. The restaurant people who had been feeding her and who wanted to adopt her gave her a name, Sasha, but they changed their minds about keeping her when, a month later, they came to visit with her (she was staying with us in an attempt to socialize her) and I had no choice but to report that her fear of humans showed no signs of subsiding, not even a little bit. So her temporary stay at our place became permanent. It wasn't all sugar 'n spice, but—as you may have noticed from the dedication page—her tiny paws left indelible prints on my heart. You'll find the rest of her story at the end of this book.

Chapter 6

Euthanasia

It's inevitable. If you get involved with rescuing, sooner rather than later you'll have to face impossible decisions—and none more so than the euthanasia call.

What if Tiny Dog (*aka* Sasha) had been older, weaker, hadn't found the restaurant people who catered so diligently to her foodstuff whims? What if one of her many illnesses had taken a greater toll? What if the vet had, upon finishing her examination, given me The Look, that serious-tinged-with-pity look every rescuer dreads? What if after a week (or a month) of treatment, instead of improving, she'd become sicker—stopped eating, showed signs of being in pain?

No one wants to choose death. Every vet I know hates having to put a dog down. The heart of every rescuer I know falls to pieces every time a life must be ended. We rescue because we have hope: that the dog can be healthy again, that s/he will find a good home, a good family. A happy ending. But sometimes the happiest ending possible is an end to the pain. A death with dignity, in the hands of someone who cares enough to give it to you. That someone, dear rescuer, is you. There's no one else. This dog is completely alone in the world—except for you. And s/he needs you to make the right choice. Understand this: rescue isn't so much about *saving lives* as it is about *guaranteeing quality of life*. So put your heartbreak aside—this isn't about you, remember?—and focus on doing what's best for the dog.

The decision to put a dog down isn't one made lightly. Not by vets, not by the rescuers who bring them in. All sorts of considerations go into it, and, because dogs—just like humans—are individuals with individual health scenarios and individual capabilities for strength, no two cases are alike.

Disease

If the dog has a too-advanced case of an incapacitating, or even deadly, disease such as distemper or parvovirus (this latter mostly in puppies), their chances of survival—and for quality of life even if they do survive—become close to nil. The vet might suggest putting them on an IV drip overnight to see if they respond, but sometimes the dog's illness is so advanced, and the potential for recovery or even relief so small, that the recommendation will be to euthanize immediately.

More on diseases in *Health Issues* (p. 63).

Pain

Dogs have a broader threshold for pain than humans, so injuries or conditions that might look unbearably painful to us may not necessarily be so for the dog. Your vet is the most qualified to assess the dog's level of pain, and to judge whether it's causing serious suffering. If it's something that can be alleviated quickly, say via meds or surgery, chances are your vet will recommend a course of treatment. If it can't, or if the dog's chances of recovery are slim, then you'll need to make a decision. No one wants to condemn a dog to a lifetime of pain.

Resources

This is the eternal bane of rescue: *do we have the resources we need to save this dog?* Sometimes the disease might be cured by long-term treatment, the injury fixed with sophisticated surgeries, the pain alleviated through therapy... But all these things cost money. And, more than money, they also require dedicated caretakers. With shelters full, foster homes in short supply, and rescue organizations already operating far beyond their capacity, sometimes it comes down to choosing between saving this one life or saving three, five, ten others.

You can imagine how difficult—how utterly devastating—it is for a rescuer to make the euthanasia call in these scenarios. These are the times when the unfairness of it all hits the hardest... Practical reasons fall on deaf ears for the heart (and the soul).

Attitude

Not yours; the dog's. Some dogs come in with comparatively minor issues, but their spirit is no longer willing to fight. They look up at you from the examining table with eyes that plead for release. *I've had it. Let me go.* Some of these dogs might be saved still, especially if their medical issues aren't too severe—and nothing is as gratifying as watching that spirit come back when the meds start working and the body starts healing—but, if the disease or injury is serious and the vet is recommending euthanasia, these are dogs who are ready to go. Give them that last kindness, and set them free.

On the other hand, I've seen X-rays that tell a horrific story: compound hip or spine fractures, tissue shredded, bones splintered into impossible puzzles. One expects to find that dog prone, immobile, if not outright unconscious. Instead, what you find is a dog who's not just mobile but *happy*. The will to live shines in their eyes, in their eagerness to get up, to greet you, to show you they're up for the challenge. Their tail wags and you hear it loud and clear: *bring it on*. For those dogs, you'll see rescuers go to the ends of the earth. Bank accounts get emptied, rent doesn't get paid, fundraising campaigns flood social media.

Listen to the dog.

Consensus

No one should, or should have to, make the euthanasia call on their own. If you're part of a rescue organization, you'll have all the support (and input, and second—and third—opinions) you need. If you're a lone rescuer, make sure you have (on speed dial) a good, animal-loving friend, preferably with at least some rescuing experience, whom you can talk it over with, who might provide new insights or perspective. Even if it's someone without any experience, someone who's never even owned a dog, they'll be able to provide a good sounding board for your reasoning and your doubts. And, if nothing else, they'll give you a shoulder to cry on. (You might need that more than anything else.)

The bottom line is that the decision to put a dog down—to end a life, to take away the possibility of hope—is never easy. No one said it should be. Quite the contrary, in fact: we all agree it should *never* be an easy thing to do. It deserves the most careful, conscientious consideration. It deserves—and requires—your whole heart.

Maybe that's why it hurts so much.

Chapter 7

Food!

Breaking bread is a ritual of friendship and respect even for us uncouth and clueless humans. Granted, instead of going around throwing pieces of sausage to the people we'd like to be friends with, we sit together at a table with cutlery and wine and candles—but, at its core, the statement of sharing (and providing) food is just as powerful: *I mean you no harm. I'm on your side.*

Food is a powerful ally for dog rescuers. Well, it *can* be. If you've already read *Catch Me If You Can* (p. 34), you know even something as friendly as food is nowhere near fail-safe.

The Bait

Forget dog kibble. Ferals and long-time strays forage for their meals in our trash, and the finest kibble will never match the appeal of a discarded half-eaten burger, or even the cleanest-picked chicken bone.

So use those. (Not the bones. *Dogs should never, ever get bones, especially not chicken.*)[4] Sausage, liverwurst, chicken livers, ham, cheese, or any other kind of yummy (cooked) meat... Okay, you get the idea.

Wait, no, don't use a whole steak. What do you think will happen when feral, skinny, famished dog lands a huge, juicy steak? First thing s/he'll do is run off to a safe place to eat it. *Safe*, by the way, meaning *out of sight*. Sure, s/he might come back for

---

[4] Bones, especially when cooked, tend to splinter when broken. These splinters may lodge in the dog's throat, stomach, or intestines, causing bleeding, perforation, and even death.

more eventually, but not until s/he's slept it off: his/her reduced stomach will need a boa nap to digest this unexpected windfall of protein and fat.

Whatever goody you've chosen, cut it up into pieces no larger than the size of your fingertip. Yes, it's a messy job. Include baby wipes in your *Dog Rescue Kit* (see p. 85).

The How

Your Goal

Get the dog to approach you—or let you approach them. Food is your negotiation tool. Careful, though: this is about trust. Don't make it a "come closer and you'll get more" kind of conversation. The dog will sense ulterior motives, so make it easy on everyone and be upfront about what you want. *Yes, I want to touch you.* Food is not a distraction; it's a reward, a token of your goodwill.

Remember Your Manners

Don't look them in the eye. Sit on the ground to take away some of that scary human uprightness, and don't face them head-on: letting them approach you a little from the side makes you less intimidating.

Throw a couple of pieces (softly; remember the dog has probably had stones thrown at him/her, and you really don't want to fall into that category of two-legged monster) in the dog's general direction. Depending on the level of his/her fear, you might not want to aim your first throws in the dog's immediate space; throw diagonally, close enough to them so s/he can catch a whiff of whatever goody you're using and identify it as food, without feeling threatened.

Once the dog eats the first two or three, you'll know both that you've chosen your bait well and that the dog is open to giving you a chance. You can now begin throwing the pieces progressively closer to you, but not too fast, and not too many (you don't want them to be full so fast; once in the car, s/he can eat as much as s/he wants). Develop a rhythm, do your best to become predictable; in Dogspeak, predictability equals trustworthiness.

Take time to read the dog; when s/he hesitates, throw one or two pieces nearer to them again, and wait until those go down the hatch before you continue shortening the "bread-crumb" path.

Get the Dog to Eat From Your Hand

When the dog is close enough, offer him/her a piece from your open palm. Holding it in your fingers is inviting the dog to snatch it; s/he might miscalculate, take a bit of finger along. Which will make you snatch your hand back—and that burst of movement, as well as your burst of adrenaline, will drive the dog right back to where you lured him/her from. (Remember when we said about getting hurt being only important in the measure in which it affects Getting The Dog?)

Keep your hand below their nose level, and move slowly. Not hesitating, just slowly. Smoothly. Breathe. If you want this dog to trust you, you'll need to trust yourself, too.

If s/he seems unwilling to take it, set it down on the ground where s/he'll feel safer—and validate that safety by not attempting to sneak in a touch or a grab. Then, when they've eaten that one, offer another piece in your hand again. Repeat until s/he takes it from you. After one or two more pieces, you can try touching. When s/he takes the piece from your hand, touch his/her chin with your fingers—which is another reason why you offer food from your open palm: you want to keep your fingertips free for that 'accidental' brush on the dog's chin.

When the dog seems comfortable with your touch, especially if s/he allows you to touch the top of his/her head, you're ready for the leash. Have it ready, and slip it on smoothly: no jerky or sudden movements. You're in charge, you know what you're doing and that what you're doing is a *good* thing, and the dog will sense all this from the steadiness of your hand.

The Leash is On. Now What?

Take a moment to congratulate yourself—you did it! Breathe, revel in the joy: thanks to you, this little guy is on the road to safety. But don't get up just yet; your job isn't quite finished. If you read *Catch Me If You Can* (p. 34), you know the leash is often what sets off a panic. So don't rush.

And don't put away the goodies.

For everything that the dog allows from you—every touch, every pat, and certainly the leash around his/her neck—s/he should get another piece of sausage, cheese, whatever you're using. It's not just a reward; it's also the reiteration of this covenant you're in the process of making: *I take care of you, you can trust me.* Once the leash is on, you'll have a better chance of avoiding that fighting, panicky mode if you give the dog enough time and space to accept this.

The Routine

What if it doesn't work, though? What if, no matter the quality of the goodies you use, the dog won't take more than two or three pieces before bolting? What if, like Tiny Dog, s/he will eat eagerly but, no matter how you beg and plead, won't come close enough to hand-feed or to touch?

When a dog has proved too skittish for a short-term lure, and assuming you (and the dog) have the time—i.e. there's no urgency, whether medical or situational—another option is to create a feeding routine. Over the course of days, weeks, and even months, you'll establish a feeding ritual—much like the one you have with your dogs at home. The goal is to get the dog to come to the same place at the same time every day (yes, including weekends), get him/her to associate you with food and safety, and get used to your presence.

Your goal here might be working up to touch him/her, eventually—or, for very fearful dogs, to plan the use of more drastic capture methods (like traps, or drugs), for which you need to be able to predict the dog's location at least at one given time of day.

There are also cases when the dog can't be rescued, for any number of reasons: lack of fosters, no shelter space, traps and drugs have been tried and failed. A feeding routine is often the only way to care for these dogs. If the routine is working—i.e. it's firmly established—it might even provide a way of administering medical treatment.

But these feeding routines have a problem, and it's not just that they're so time-consuming. In order for them to work, you need to become the dog's primary source of food. If the dog is getting fed elsewhere, s/he might or might not show up. Which means you'll need to find those other sources of food and figure out how to eliminate them. It might be a kind person, who might be willing to help with your rescue (or—dare we hope—adopt the dog?), but it'll be one heck of a one-sided conversation if your "opponent" is, say, a restaurant trash bin.

Chapter 8
The Gratitude Myth

People often think a rescued dog will be more "grateful", and therefore more loyal, than other dogs. While that may sometimes appear to be true, it's not always the case. In my (totally biased and uneducated) opinion, a dog's loyalty—and (appearance of) gratitude—has more to do with the dog's character than with the fact s/he was rescued. Whether you agree with that or not, we can at least agree on this: there are exceptions. If a dog's gratitude is your reason for getting involved in rescue, consider this your fair warning.

Most rescued dogs adapt back into sharing their lives with humans pretty fast. The bond between us goes back a long, long way, after all: it's estimated that, although the domesticated dog probably appeared sometime between 15,000 and 30,000 years ago, the transition of wolves into their tamer cousins began around 100,000 years ago.[5] We domesticated them, but they also domesticated us: it's in their genes to love us, and to put up with our cluelessness. Even dogs who have been abused will respond favorably when rehomed to a better, kinder, environment.

Most of the time.

What self-respecting family doesn't have a problem kid (or three)? A black sheep, an unmanageable dissident? These Rebels Without A Cause happen, too, in the dog world. No matter how you try to explain it, they'll never understand that what you're doing—what you're *trying* to do—is for their own good. They'll never trust you, not completely. Often, rescue dogs are escape artists, impossible to enclose. Remember that dog

---

[5] http://dogs.about.com/od/caringfordogsandpuppies/qt/human_canine_bond.htm

who dragged her rescuer across a beach of rocks? She also chewed her way out of an "escape-proof" Sky Kennel. Or they might come with phobias: of humans, of men, of men with hats, of cars, of open spaces, of enclosed spaces, of cameras, of garden hoses, of loud sounds, of... Well. You name it. Or they might be protective, territorial. They might not get along with other dogs. Or with children. Or be forever suspicious of any visitor. Or even of you.

We have no way of knowing what these dogs have gone through. The things they had to learn in order to survive—the things that made them renegades. Dogs perceive the world very differently; they're more sensitive, more observant. They see— hear, smell, feel—things that our overloaded and atrophied human senses don't even register. Lisel Mueller puts it beautifully in her poem, *What The Dog Perhaps Hears*.

> What is it like up there
> above the shut-off level
> of our simple ears?
> For us there was no birth cry,
> the newborn bird is suddenly here,
> the egg broken, the nest alive,
> and we heard nothing when the world changed.

Born in the street, or abandoned at an early age, a dog has little exposure (if any) to positive human interaction. We've become the enemy: the tall, loud, aggressive creatures that throw stones, that shout, that tease with the promise of food, that hurt when we touch. Can you blame them for distrusting us?

But these renegades also need a home. They need love, *human* love—even if they don't know they do, or don't know how to ask for it. And it takes the rarest breed of human to give it to them.

Most people, when they adopt (or otherwise acquire) a dog, do so with explicit (and implicit) expectations. They're looking for a playmate for their kids, or a quiet companion that will fill an emptying nest, or an exercise partner, or a security asset, or an imposing specimen that will reinforce their social status. They come to the shelters already envisioning the life this new family member will enable, or enhance. And very, very few are willing to readjust that vision, even let go of it altogether, to save a growling, wary dog who looks more like s/he wants to have you for dinner than cuddle with you.

That's assuming you even get to see them. A shy, angsty dog—who maybe doesn't get along with other dogs, who maybe has a special fear of men or kids, or has any other number of behavior issues—won't likely be among the options paraded in shelter yards for shiny happy families looking to adopt. (And when these shiny happy people do adopt them—maybe they fell in love with the dog and insisted on "giving it a try", maybe the shelter didn't assess the dog properly, or the adoption is being handled by an inexperienced employee—it tends to end in tragedy: a bitten child, an attack on the postman or a neighbor, wrecked living rooms... And the dog, once again, behind bars—or in the street.)

How ironic, then, that these rebels—who have, because of their rebelliousness, the least possibilities of getting adopted—are the ones in the direst need of a home. The system doesn't work in their favor: they'll probably live out their lives in a four-by-four cage, with minimal interaction with humans or other dogs. And, at kill shelters, they're at the highest risk for euthanasia.

Every once in a while, not nearly often enough but maybe, just maybe, in the nick of time for this one lucky dog, a special someone will show up. Perhaps it's a rescue organization with the resources and the experience (and, above all, the dedication) to rehabilitate the dog. Perhaps—and these are my favorite stories—it's just someone, a regular someone to all (apparent) effects and purposes, maybe someone who's never even owned a dog, but who has a size XXL heart. And... magic happens.

"He's... difficult," the shelter employee says. "We have some other dogs in the—"

But the man is already kneeling by the cage. "What happened to him?"

"We don't know. He came in a couple of weeks ago, in really bad shape."

The dog is sitting at the back of the cage, facing the wall. Thick grey-black fur, so matted that it'll have to be shaved off, doesn't quite disguise the bony ribs beneath. At the sound of the voices, his head hunkers further down, as if all he wants is to disappear, to become invisible.

"Can I go inside?" the man asks.

The shelter employee is unsure; there have been some incidents. He's a big dog, after all. She tries to point the man in the direction of other, friendlier, dogs, but the man insists. They make an appointment for the next day; the resident behaviorist will be in then.

Over the next week, man and dog get to know each other. The behaviorist chokes up the day the dog finally—*finally!*—approaches the man, crawling, trembling, and with the faintest hint of a wagging movement at the tip of his dreadlocked tail. They bring the dog to the man's home for a visit the next day; the brand-new two-meter fence meets the shelter's require-ments, but the dog completely ignores the pile of toys laid out for him.

"Give him time," the behaviorist tells the man, and writes down the number of a trainer friend who's helped out with severe cases adopted from the shelter before. When he calls—as soon as the shelter people are gone and he and the dog are alone—the trainer tells him she'll come by tomorrow. But she warns him not to expect miracles.

"That's not what training is about," she says. "It's about establishing the basics of communication between you two. This dog is... who he is. He might get better, he might not. But he's begun to trust you. Don't betray that trust by trying to make him into someone he's not."

Maybe this man knows all about being made into something you're not. Maybe he has some close-up-and-personal experience with failing to meet expectations. Maybe he's just an empathetic soul. In any case, he understands. He doesn't push, he doesn't press. He lets the dog take the lead on how much love, and how often, and when. He respects. And, through training, he learns to communicate that respect to the dog. He lets the dog know he can be trusted to protect and to guide. In other words, he lets the dog *be*.

~ * ~

The bottom line is that a rescued dog won't necessarily, or "gratefully", fade into the wallpaper of your life. Rescue dogs often need both more and less human interaction. More because they'll need behavior training—focused, tailored, more positive reinforcement. Less because they'll need more space. More patience. You'll need to move slower in gaining their trust. You'll need to keep goals realistic, and minimal. And each tiny step forward will be cause for celebration.

Whether you're a rescuer finding a family for a fearful, angsty dog or looking to adopt one yourself, remember that it's all about setting the dog up for success. The best home for a renegade dog will be with people who are open-minded, who have few preconceptions about what a dog should be like. Who are willing to put the dog first, and adapt their lives to him/her.

And it's not only about behavior. Even the friendliest, most outgoing rescue dog might have health issues that will become a challenge for the family that adopts him/her.

Chapter 9
Health Issues

You don't need a degree in veterinary medicine to become a dog rescuer. But, whether by choice or necessity, once you start rescuing you'll end up learning at least the basics of canine health.

Chances are that any dog you pick up in the street will have health issues. If you (and s/he) are lucky, they'll be minor. But if the dog is either a feral or has been on the street for a while, the odds don't really favor luck.

Some people seem to think strays—mutts, non-breeds—are predisposed to illness, that they have some sort of physiological weakness that makes them more vulnerable to disease than, say, purebred dogs. It's actually the other way around: street dogs, especially ferals, tend to have solid immune systems. The street is a tough place, and it takes extraordinary physiology to survive there. Plus, dogs that breed out of controlled environments have a huge gene pool, whereas pedigreed animals are, by definition, limited to a reduced selection.

No, strays aren't weak or somehow defective; quite the contrary: they are the *crème de la crème* of natural selection. The strongest, the fittest, the most able to adapt. I get how that might be hard to believe when faced with a dog that's nothing but fur and bones (and not even that much fur) but—please, give credit where credit is due. The street is not exactly a hospitable environment for life to thrive: unlike family dogs, strays are exposed to all sorts of dangers, visible (vehicles, human cruelty) and invisible (bacteria and viruses), and they receive no preventive care at all. The fact that they made it long enough for you to find them makes them something like Superdogs.

Which is why your first stop, once you have the dog in the car, and—especially—before you take him/her home, is at the vet's. This might be obvious if you've rescued a dog who's just been hit by a car, for instance, or one with visible wounds. But even when the dog looks relatively okay, remember this: *because* they're Superdogs, disease won't be evident to the untrained eye until it's in advanced stages. A family dog might lose his/her appetite or be less active at the first symptoms of illness; a street dog will most likely hide any signs of weakness until they're literally unable to. And by then it might be too late.

So. Do yourself—and the dog—a favor and go straight to the vet. There are silent killers afoot.

These are some of the issues you'll come across:

Parasites

Ticks

A stray dog without ticks is... well, not a stray. They reproduce prodigiously, they can withstand all sorts of hostile environments, they survive for years without hosts, and they're impossible for a dog to fight off on his/her own. As a rescuer, you'll soon get used to the sight of tick-infested dogs: whole colonies in the ears, between the toes, around the eyes.

I know. Disgusting. And those huge populations of ticks represent a serious loss of blood for a dog—serious enough to cause anemia (see *Anemia* on p. 73). But these creatures aren't just revolting bloodsuckers, they also transmit nasty diseases. The brown dog tick, for instance, which is the one most commonly found on dogs here in Curaçao and in the US, transmits *ehrlichiosis* (also known as *tick fever, canine hemorrhagic fever, canine typhus,* and a host of other names): a life-threatening infection caused by bacteria[6] called *Ehrlichia*, after German microbiologist Paul Ehrlich. These bacteria reproduce in white blood cells, which aren't just found in blood but also in bone marrow, the liver, the spleen, and lymph nodes. These last three will often be enlarged in animals with ehrlichiosis, and their function impaired. One of the most serious consequences is that, by suppressing the function of bone marrow, ehrlichiosis causes disruption in the production of new red and white blood cells.

Ehrlichia also destroy platelets, the cells in blood responsible for coagulation or clotting, which will produce abnormal bleeding (hence the name *hemorrhagic fever*). Surgery—or any procedure that involves bleeding—on a dog positive for ehrlichiosis is a bad, bad idea, and a vet will only risk it in urgent cases.

Once the disease reaches chronic stage (the case of most ferals or long-time strays), the damage to the dog's entire physiology is irreversible—and, eventually, fatal.

Diagnosing ehrlichiosis

Blood testing will tell the vet whether the dog has been exposed to Ehrlichia. But diagnosing the stage of the illness, outside of the terminal cases, is much more difficult. An experienced vet will be able to narrow it down by taking the blood test results in the context of their clinical exam and visual observations.

Treatment

Getting rid of the ticks is the easy part; I've had extraordinary success with chewable tablets, but tick control medications come in all forms, sizes, and budgets. For a rescue, though, it's doubly important that you consult with your vet to make sure the product you use doesn't contain ingredients that may amplify or otherwise worsen any other medical issues. No

---

[6] Some sources classify Ehrlichia as a *rickettsia*, an organism sort of in between bacteria and viruses.

matter how safe the product is stated to be, it *is* poison of a kind, which means a severely ill animal may not be able to handle it.

Treating the ehrlichiosis will be more of a challenge. The vet will probably prescribe oral antibiotics such as tetracycline, but—depending on the severity of the case—perhaps the dog will require IV fluids or even blood transfusions. Additional treatment may include prednisone (a corticosteroid) to help kickstart the bone marrow's blood cell production, or perhaps vitamin K as a blood-clotting aid.

In short, as common as ehrlichiosis is, each case is different, and requires a medical professional not just to diagnose but to treat effectively.

Fleas

As prevalent as ticks, and just as hard for a dog to deal with on his/her own. Out-of-control flea populations will cause enough blood loss to result in anemia, much more often than ticks do, but even in smaller numbers they produce skin irritations which, if left untreated, can get bad enough to look like mange, and cause enormous discomfort to the dog.

But that's not the worst of it. Fleas may not transmit ehrlichiosis, but they *do* transmit tapeworms. These parasites live in the dog's small intestine, and they consume nutrients as they pass through, thus causing weight loss and nutritional deficiency. Tapeworm is a priority in treatment, because as long as they're present any oral medication the dog receives— anything s/he eats, actually—will only partially make it into their body, making it less effective.

Treatment

Giving the dog a bath might be your first instinct, and although that's usually a good idea, do take into consideration that anti-flea shampoos tend to be rather aggressive. If the dog has severe skin irritation, you'll want to check with the vet first. The age of the dog also plays a role, as does their overall health.

Most tick control medication also works against fleas, and once the fleas are gone the dermatitis will disappear as well, though hair may take longer to grow back in. A vet may also recommend using special medicated shampoos, not to fight the fleas but to soothe the skin and help it heal.

It'll be the tapeworms that most concern you. The dog will need to receive deworming medication, usually two weeks apart, to get rid of that problem. And, depending on the severity of the anemia, additional supplements may be prescribed. (See below.)

Lice

Much less common than ticks or fleas. It's actually rather rare for a family dog to get lice; many dog owners don't even know that dog lice exists. That's because they thrive in extremely unsanitary conditions (think garbage dumps).

There are two types of lice: skin-eating, and blood-sucking. Both types are transmitted by direct contact with either another dog who has them or with contaminated objects (sleeping areas, fabric, etc). The good news for you, though, is that lice are species-specific parasites, which means you won't get them. (And, if you happened to have human lice, your dog couldn't get them from you.)

Like ticks and fleas, a large infestation of blood-sucking lice will result in anemia for the dog. They don't usually cause allergies, unlike fleas, but the biting does cause itching (obviously), which results in hair loss and patchy, scabby skin. These scabs may get infected, especially given the unsanitary conditions, which may bring on a whole other host of problems.

Treatment

Because a dog with lice will be predictably filthy, a bath is usually the top priority. But—I can't stress this enough—check with the vet for the right shampoo and ask about any other risks or considerations. Tick and flea control products may work against lice—but there may be drawbacks. In long-haired dogs, especially if their coats are matted, it's usually necessary to shave off the fur to get rid of the lice nits (eggs).

Heartworm Disease

The parasite is called *Dirofilaria immitis*, and its larvae, transmitted by mosquitoes, enter the bloodstream and lodge in the larger vessels of the cardiovascular system and in the heart, eventually multiplying and causing serious damage—often irreversible, even after the parasite is eliminated. As with ehrlichiosis, a dog diagnosed with heartworms is a poor candidate for any kind of surgical intervention.

Dirofilaria is a silent, sneaky, progressive killer, and invisible to boot. Even dogs who have lived with heartworms for years will often present no observable signs at all. The only way to detect it is via blood test.

Treatment

Varies according to the severity of the case (and the overall health of the dog), but it usually involves Immiticide (Melarsomine), a compound that contains arsenic. The dog receives three injections, the first two a month apart and the third 24 hours after the second. They're very painful, not just the injections themselves (they're given after a preparatory pain med) but also the effect of the drug itself, which lasts between six and twelve hours.

Immiticide comes with risks of its own: as the worms die, they will dislodge and travel along blood vessels, raising the possibility of embolisms. The vet will recommend strict rest for the dog during 4 to 6 weeks after treatment, to reduce this possibility, but make no mistake: this is an aggressive treatment which may cause damage to kidneys and lungs, and may even kill the dog. The vet will weigh very carefully the risk of using it against the risk of *not* using it—but heartworm disease will always, in every case, kill the dog. Immiticide, with all its hazards, may still be the only hope.

As if heartworms weren't deadly enough already, they also bring *Wolbachia*, bacteria that infect the worms themselves, into the dog's body and which causes inflammation. This is why heart worm disease treatment most often includes simultaneous high doses of antibiotics as well.

Viral Diseases

Parvovirus
Usually affects only the very young: once a dog is over a year old, his/her parvo risks diminish markedly. Sometimes, however, senior dogs with compromised immune systems are susceptible to the virus—as may be the case of rescues, abandoned or feral. The disease affects fast-growing cells, such as those found in the intestines or the blood; survivors—which are mighty rare—often end up with long-term cardiac issues. *Very* contagious, especially through contact with infected feces and vomit. If you suspect a dog might have parvo (not eating, vomiting, bloody diarrhea), be sure to disinfect any of your skin that came into contact with him/her with alcohol, the soles of your shoes and any other non-organic surface with bleach, and wash your clothes with a fabric-safe but powerful disinfectant. And make sure your dogs at home are current on their vaccines.

Diagnosing Parvovirus
A vet will diagnose based on a clinical exam and testing a stool sample. The ELISA test, which makes use of enzymes, is fast but not 100% specific, so the vet may want to do other tests.

Treatment
Being viral, no cure is available; treatment relies on controlling symptoms and boosting the dog's defenses until his/her own immune system itself beats the virus: hospitalization, IV drip, antibiotics, anti-vomit meds, anti-seizure meds, etc. During treatment and until declared otherwise by a vet, any dog

infected (or suspected of being infected) with parvo (or distemper; see next section) *must be isolated from other dogs*. If you're caring for the dog, you need to disinfect yourself, your clothes, shoes, watch, jewelry, steering wheel, car upholstery, door handles, etc, before having contact with other animals.

If the case is too advanced and the dog does not respond to treatment, euthanasia is the most humane resolution; both parvovirus and distemper, left on their own, end in a horrible, painful death.

Distemper

Unlike parvo, distemper doesn't discriminate by age or by anything else. It attacks the respiratory, nervous, gastro-intestinal, and urogenital systems, as well as lymph nodes. Especially in advanced stages, you'll see seizures, paralysis, hobbled walking, nervous "tics", hysteria. It's *very* contagious (it's airborne). As with parvo, disinfect everything that might have come into contact with a potentially infected dog, and make sure your own dogs are up to date on their vaccines.

Diagnosing Distemper

Via biochemical tests and urine analysis. Depending on the stage of the disease, epithelial cells may be tested for antibodies, and radiographs and CT and MRI scans can be used to determine the extent of neurological damage. Where these high-tech options aren't available (such as, say, in Curaçao), vets have become experts at watching for symptoms, and developing hands-on reflex assessments to test abnormal neurological responses.

Treatment

See parvovirus *Treatment* section (p. 69).

Rabies

A viral infection that causes brain swelling (*polioencephalitis*). Transmissible via blood or saliva (most commonly by bite), and is exceptionally deadly. Only six humans have survived rabies. I could find no record of any dog surviving it. In Curaçao, as in many small islands, rabies has been eradicated; we don't even vaccinate for it (unless the dog is going to Europe or the U.S.). One less thing to worry about here when catching a stray dog. This does mean, though, that my experience with rabies is mighty limited. If you live in an area where rabies is a risk, please check with local (experienced) rescuers before coming into contact with a dog you suspect of being infected with rabies. Rabid dogs exhibit atypical behavior, which makes them unpredictable. When possible, it's best to leave their capture to animal control or other competent professionals.

Diagnosing Rabies
When an animal is suspected of having been infected, s/he will be quarantined for observation (up to six months in some places). If the animal dies while quarantined, the veterinarian (or, in some places, the disease control authorities) will perform a post-mortem test to confirm the diagnosis.

Treatment
None, really. If a dog has been vaccinated, s/he has a chance of fighting the disease. Rabies, however, is *always* fatal for unvaccinated dogs.

TVTs (Transmissible Venereal Tumors)
Otherwise known as histiocytic tumors, one of the rare kinds of transmissible cancers. The tumor cells are themselves the infectious agents, and the tumors that form are not genetically related to the 'host'. They seldom metastasize to other organs, and are rarely life-threatening. Usually transmitted via sexual contact, the reason why they're most often seen in the genital area, but they may also occur on noses or mouths.

Treatment

Surgery isn't recommended; due to its nature, the tumor has excellent chances of growing back after removal. Additionally, the areas it affects (genitals, mucous membranes) provide narrow margins to guarantee effective extirpation. Chemotherapy is much more successful, usually via an agent called *vincristine* and dispensed intravenously once a week for four weeks. After the first chemo treatment, bleeding in the tumor stops. By the fourth, the tumor has either disappeared or has shrunk to near-invisiblity. Sometimes a fifth round might be prescribed, but if the tumor is still present after that, chances are it wasn't a TVT at all, and more testing will be necessary.

Skin Issues (Mange)

Caused by microscopic mites, external parasites that feed on skin. Most mites are part of a dog's skin, but can cause irritation if populations get out of hand: hair loss, scabby-looking skin, dry and red patches.

Sarcoptic Mange (or Scabies)

Highly contagious to other dogs *and humans*. Mites burrow through skin causing intense itching; the scratching is what produces the symptoms (hair loss, scabs, rashes, etc).

Treatment

The dog must be isolated from other dogs. If you're caring for him/her, be sure to wash hands and all exposed skin as well as clothes thoroughly before coming into contact with other animals. Treatment, which typically lasts several weeks, includes scabicide drugs via injection, sometimes paired with oral medication—usually antibiotics to fight secondary bacterial skin infections. The younger the dog, the more effective (and fast-working) the treatment will be.

Demodectic Mange (Demodicosis / Demodex)

Non-contagious. Demodectic mange mites are normally present in a dog's skin and only become a problem when population becomes too large (apparently a genetic issue). May be localized, which is common in puppies and will resolve itself naturally, or generalized, which tend to become more severe (dramatic hair loss, skin wounds from scratching, etc).

Treatment:

Due to its genetic nature, demodicosis is treated very differently from sarcoptic mange: scabicides won't work, but other dips or shampoos may help soothe irritation (and prevent excessive scratching, which is 90% of the problem). Treatment is usually long-term (think months instead of weeks), though it really can vary, from localized lesions that resolve themselves as the dog's immune system matures, to lifelong treatment to keep the mite population under control.

Overall Health Concerns

Anemia

In strays or feral dogs, it's most often a consequence of parasites, whether internal or external, paired with a poor, nutrient-deficient diet.

Treatment

The vet will probably prescribe nutritional supplements, such as Lixotinic (rich in iron, copper, B-complex vitamins, and essential amino acids) or Meg-A-Cal (high-calorie, high-fat, plus vitamins), along with a balanced diet. In severe cases, a shot of vitamins or even an overnight IV may provide a much-needed boost.

Dehydration

Usually present in dogs suffering from some kind of digestive problem (parvovirus, for instance, or advanced infestation of intestinal parasites). But relatively healthy dogs may show signs of dehydration; in hot and dry climates, homeless animals have a very hard time finding water.

Treatment

Mild cases will be solved within a day or two once the dog has a regular source of drinking water, but in severe cases, or when there are other medical conditions present, the vet may want to put the dog on an IV for a couple of hours or even overnight.

Dental Concerns

Build-up on teeth is typically grotesque in homeless dogs, especially if they're older, and causes painful gums that often prevent him/her from eating. Beyond the gums, however, is something potentially deadly: the bacteria that hide in all that build-up regularly spread to heart valves, causing inflammation—and heart disease. (Have you checked your dog's teeth lately?)

Treatment

Professional tooth cleaning. However, because there will be bleeding involved, if the dog tests positive for ehrlichiosis or heartworm disease, or even just anemia, you'll need to work with the vet on deciding when to do this procedure. Chances are there will be more urgent issues to take care of first. Also, the amount of bacteria in the mouth—especially one belonging to a stray or feral dog—is not just high but of particular strength, too, which means the dog will probably need a round of antibiotics before, and maybe even after, the tooth cleaning takes place.

Arthrosis

A non-inflammatory affliction of the joints caused by normal wear and tear, usually seen in senior dogs.

Treatment

There is no cure, but symptoms can easily be treated with pain meds.

Rescue dogs, regardless of age or time in the street, may present any (or all) of the above in wildly creative combinations and variables of strength and severity. But this is only a general outlook. Depending on where you live (and rescue), some of these diseases may not apply, or even exist—and some different ones may. Add to that the 'minor' (in comparison) considerations of vitamin and/or amino acid deficiencies which most street dogs suffer and which can cause a wide range of symptoms, diseases, and malformations that will impact the dog's health long after they're off the street, and you begin to understand why there's absolutely no excuse for not bringing a rescue dog *straight* to the vet. You pick up a dog, you bring him/her to the vet. It's that simple. And it's that important.

Chapter 10
The Immensity of It All

Rescue is not for sissies.

Health care professionals, social workers, people who work at child care facilities or nursing homes: what do all these have in common? They're the jobs most often associated with depression.[7] Did you know this? I didn't. But maybe I should've. Seems fairly obvious.

Something else that's obvious: the similarities between these professions and animal rescue. Looking after sick or otherwise incapacitated people—*check*—who can't (or won't) show appreciation or speak up for themselves—*check*—and who are often victims, whether of abuse or cruelty or just situations they have very little control over—*check*. Feelings of helplessness—*check*—and a culture that equates success with sacrifice—*check*.

Animal rescue may not be a *job*—there's certainly no monetary gain in it (the opposite, in fact) or opportunities for career growth—but it's just as draining, psychologically and emotionally, as any of these professions.

There's the cruelty, for instance. Like social workers, rescuers see more of it on a daily basis than the average person sees in their entire lifetime. Dogs abandoned in the wild, tied to a tree, without water or food. Newborn puppies left to die in a cardboard box by the side of the road. Dogs with rope (or even wire!) wrapped so tight their whole necks have become an open, suppurating wound. Dogs with fear in their eyes, who cower and flinch at your touch.

---

7 http://www.health.com/health/gallery/0,,20428990,00.html

There's the indifference. The way people keep buying from pet stores and breeders when shelters are all overflowing with unwanted dogs. The way they turn a blind eye to the skinny, mangy dogs in their neighborhood. How they 'forget' to sterilize their pets. Or how they move away and leave them behind.

And then people wonder why rescuers become 'anti-social'.

Then there are the tough decisions. The dogs found too late, so far gone that your only option is to offer an end to the pain, a dignified death in the hands of a few humans who care. The pregnancies terminated because—well, because there are already too many (way, *way* too many) homeless dogs.

These are all low, low points in a rescuer's life, but they're not the worst. What gets you—all of us, sooner or later—is the immensity of the problem.

At some point in every dog rescuer's path comes a moment when you realize you can't save all the dogs. You can't even save the majority. In fact, you and all the rescuers of the world are engaged in the deranged task of emptying an endless, ever-growing ocean—*and you're doing it with fucking eyedroppers.*

The day that moment happens is... well, not a pretty day.

So. Should you quit? Avoid getting involved from the outset? Sounds like the reasonable, intelligent thing to do, right? Except... What if you're losing sleep over that all-bones dog you saw slinking around the neighborhood yesterday? Face it, cowboy: at your core, you're a dog rescuer. And denying it will make you miserable. Your conscience won't let up, you'll never have peace, not until you *do* something.

What you need, then, is to figure out a way to keep this immensity from taking over, from tainting all your rescues, from tipping you head-first into the bottomless pit of despair.

How does a rescuer find perspective?

- Celebrate every victory, no matter how small, no matter what else went wrong. In every rescue (as in *everything*) there's good and there's bad. Learn from the bad, celebrate the good. No matter how small, how insignificant it may seem. It's your choice what you magnify, what you minimize. Get into the habit of magnifying the good.

- You know what else is a great source of learning? The dogs themselves. They're survivors. They're fighters. They're resilient beyond belief. Unlike us humans, who seem to believe nothing but the perfect life is not just the only worthy goal but even our due. As if we were somehow *owed* it. A dog needs very little to be happy, to find the strength to stay alive, to *thrive* even. If you want to be happy—really, truly happy—I have only one recommendation, whether you're in rescue or not: be more *dog*.

- Collect—in a journal, in photos, on Pinterest, in a (*cough, cough*) book—the rescue stories that make your heart sing. Go back to them often, even when you're happy and don't think you need a boost. (You do. Plus, if you only revisit these stories when you're down, eventually you'll associate them with feeling low—and their magic will wear off.)

- Hang out with action-oriented people; avoid the complainers.

- Don't be a complainer yourself. Your last rescue went completely wrong? Don't go looking for commiseration. Don't wallow. (Seriously.)

- Take responsibility for your mistakes. You failed the dog, yes. It might be the first time this happens, but it certainly won't be the last. Learn from it. Self-pity helps no one—especially not your next rescue.

- Recharge your emotional batteries on a regular basis; don't wait until you're feeling weighed down. Figure out what it is that recharges you: music, friends, alone time, a particular author, a particular movie, exercise... Anything that makes your brain go into serotonin-and-endorphins mode.

- Forget about the big picture. Narrow your focus to *this dog*, the one you're chasing. The one you *can* help, right now. Yes, saving this one dog won't change the world—it'll keep on being a cruel, indifferent place for too many creatures. But it will be so *for one less creature today*.

~ * ~

In order for rescue to be effective, it needs to come from a place of light, from positive emotions. Rescue is about hope. It's about kindness, about doing the right thing—not for you, but for a helpless, voiceless animal. It's not about sacrifice, but about selflessness. It's not about pity, but about love.

Chapter 11

Jinxed!

Whenever I hear an ambulance, I touch a button. (You know, a clothes button. On something I'm wearing.) That's so the ambulance-related incident won't involve anyone I know. And I still turn the first cigarette of a new pack upside down, and make a wish. I have to smoke that cigarette last (hence the turning upside-down, so I can tell which little cancer tube that was), and the wish comes true.

I suppose we all have superstitions: knock on wood, don't talk about plans in the making to avoid jinxing them, avoiding cracks in the sidewalk or walking under ladders, blowing out all the candles on your birthday cake in one go so your wish will come true, not lighting more than three cigarettes with one match—or is it the third one that's unlucky? Can't ever keep that one straight.

Superstitions—like religion or life-after-death and other supernatural beliefs—are part of the human psyche. All cultures have them, all people believe in at least one or two, in greater or lesser degree. But do they work?

I've never received a call about someone I know having an accident after I've heard an ambulance siren. Have I touched a button every single time? I can't be sure. Maybe I just have extra careful friends who don't jump from roofs or try to pole-vault into their pools. The wishes I've made—in thirty years of smoking a pack a day—have come true in about the same ratio that they haven't. Speaking from my personal perspective, I'd have to conclude that superstitions serve the purpose of, one, giving us a (false?) sense of security, and two, of providing an extraneous source of whatever evils befall us. *Of course I'm having a bad day; I stepped on that crack in the sidewalk this morning.*

Nothing wrong with that, right? Sure, it's better to take responsibility for one's life, make things happen by action rather than depend on wishful thinking (or prayers or positive thoughts or whatever you want to call it), but—seriously, how many people do you know who *don't* do this? Let's face it: humans need our supernatural Kool-Aid, in bigger or smaller doses, to keep it together.

Except, of course, that some beliefs do us—and not just us—plenty more harm than good. Back in the Middle Ages, whether a woman could swim or not was an accepted proof of witchcraft. She was thrown into a body of water; if she sank (and, presumably, drowned), she was innocent. If she floated, she was guilty and would burn at the stake. The Bible[8] was widely used in the American South as 'divine' endorsement of slavery and the generalized inferiority of non-white people (it still is; just ask any white supremacist). With sexual diversity taking center stage in civil rights, the very same book is being used to oppose gay marriage.[9]

(Funny how the bits about acceptance and respect and *love thy neighbor* never make it into 'Bible-founded' arguments.)

If humans can treat members of our own species so atrociously, it seems only logical that dogs, having been our Number One companion animals for millennia, haven't escaped the brunt of our ignorance—with deadly consequences.

Have you ever heard of *BDS*? Black Dog Syndrome. All over the world, shelter employees wince when a black dog comes in. Care to take a guess why? *Because black dogs have less chances of being adopted.*

---

[8] Genesis 9:25-27, Ephesians 6:5, Titus 2:9
[9] Leviticus 18:22

Research results are divided; some show that color has significant impact on a dog's successful adoption, some that it doesn't. Some shelters have more success adopting out black dogs; at some shelters the euthanasia list is full of black dogs. I have no doubt that these mixed results are due to location, population, the years covered by the studies, and whether there were any BDS support groups active in the area.

Oh, yes. BDS is real enough, studies notwithstanding, that several groups have sprouted up around the world to promote black dog adoptions, and educate people in an attempt to mitigate the effect of the superstitions behind the black-dog hate.

But it's not just superstitions. Sure, there are plenty of Ghostly Black Dogs haunting the pages of folklore (often accompanied by a 'tall lady in white') all the way back to the Middle Ages, but I think this might be a symptom rather than the root of the problem. Think about it: what image is more effective in a ghost story, a black dog or a Golden Retriever? Imagine how much scarier Cujo would've been if he'd been a black Mastiff instead of a brown-and-white St. Bernard. The image of a black dog, especially a *big* black dog, supplies an aura of menace, doesn't it? And *that* is the root: it's not about the dog but about *our perception* of the dog.

Here's a newsflash: the color of a dog has nothing—I repeat, *nothing*—to do with a dog's character. To believe that is akin to believing that the color of someone's skin has an influence on whether they're good or bad people. Yeah, exactly: it's *racism*.

Which is, perhaps, the scummiest product of ignorance. Not that there's any shortage to choose from. But, every once in a while, ignorance results in some pretty hilarious stuff.

For instance:
- Are you between jobs? Scratch a dog before you go job hunting and you'll land a prime job.

- A baby licked by a dog will be a fast healer.
- Girls should pay attention to the direction a dog barks on St. Andrew's Eve (November 29th), because that's the direction her husband will come from.
- A dog sleeping with its tail straight out and paws upturned is supposed to foretell the arrival of bad news: the direction the tail is pointing indicates the direction the bad news will come from.
- Dogs are able to see ghosts—and, if kept by the bedside of the sick or the dying, will protect them from evil spirits.
- A dog howling at night is announcing death (or, at the very least, some sort of tragedy).
- In India, it's believed that a dog bite can impregnate a woman with puppies—who will then give the woman rabies.
- In France, if you step in dog poop, good luck is coming your way. But it has to be with your left foot.
- In Ireland, it's unlucky to meet a barking dog first thing in the morning.
- In Scotland, it's good luck for a stray to follow you home. Double luck points if it's a black dog. But, if it's raining, the luck quotient reverses and you need to get ready for your personal Armageddon.

I can't help but wonder how these originated. If stepping in poop were lucky, I'd be winning the Florida lottery every year, like clockwork. And what about a dog bite making you pregnant? With *puppies*?

Superstition, like any kind of magical thinking, might be anathema to rational behavior—but that doesn't mean *all* superstitions are grounded on a marsh of baloney. At least some must have sprouted from observable repetition rather than mere speculation—and, in fact, one has been linked by science to interestingly wise origins. (No, not the poop one.)

A howling dog announcing death. Sounds like something out of Conan Doyle, or Hitchcock, doesn't it? But think about this: the sense of smell in a dog is so keen that they perceive changes in hormones and bodily chemistry the way we perceive our neighbor is grilling burgers next door. Science has found out they're able to smell certain diseases on us: cancer is one, and epilepsy is another—which is why epileptic patients have service dogs specially trained to signal when an attack is coming on.

(No, the signal is *not* a bone-chilling howl.)

Chapter 12

The Dog Rescuer's Kit

The truth is you don't require much to rescue a dog. In a pinch, all you really need are your hands and a halfway working brain. (And none of the items below will be much use if you don't have those.) But there are a few things that can make your life easier.

Basics

- **Noose Leash.** The sturdy, thicker weave makes it harder for a dog to chew their way loose. Plus, the snare slides smoothly, and a leather safety ring keeps it from loosening (which happens if you just loop a regular leash).

- **Regular Leash.** Because... back-ups, dude.

- **Make-Friends Goodies** (*aka* bait). Use the irresistible stuff: sausage, liverwurst, cheese, bits of beef, etc. And remember to cut it into small, small pieces. (See *Food!*, p. 52)

- **Towels.** Truly the most useful of all possible aids. Towels have saved my rescuing ass so many different times, in so many different ways, that I couldn't begin to list them all. Beyond the obvious stuff (drying, protecting your car seats), they're great allies when dealing with skittish and/or biting dogs. Throw a towel over a terrified dog and s/he'll quiet down. Wrap one around the head of a fearful dog to protect you from bites (and him from hurting him/herself). Use as a stretcher to carry an injured dog into your car. Use as lining in transport kennels to provide better footing for your four-legged passenger. (Need I go on?) Old bedsheets work too, but, being thinner, offer less protection, and being larger, they're harder to handle fast and effectively.

- **Water Container.** And not just a water bottle. We're talking serious size here. You'll use this not just for the dog, if s/he's thirsty or needs rinsing, but also to wash yourself off. And the water needs to be fresh: you'll be storing this in your car, which—year-round here in Curaçao, during summer elsewhere—can get pretty hot, and heat makes plastic leach toxic chemicals into the container's contents.[10]

- **Disinfectant & Alcohol.** Stray and feral dogs carry all sorts of bacteria and microbes, and you won't know which ones, or, if they're sick, how contagious the disease might be, until a vet sees them. Better safe than sorry; you need to disinfect your clothing, your shoe soles, and your hands before touching, say, the steering wheel or the door handles of your car. (See *Health Issues*, p. 63)

For Your Comfort

- **Sturdy Footwear.** No sandals, no flip-flops. You'll need to run, and not necessarily along even terrain; you'll be stepping into all sorts of shit (literally); you might need to go into brush and dead branches and thorns and...

- **Disposable Gloves.** You never know what you might need to touch.

- **Gardening Gloves.** Optional, but they've come in handy for me a couple of times. (Mostly with bloodthirsty dogs.)

- **Water & an Energy Bar.** You have no way of telling how long a rescue is going to take. It might be fast, or it might take

---

[10] http://www.ncbi.nlm.nih.gov/pubmed/?term=Effects+of+storage+temperature+and+duration+on+release+of+antimony+and+bisphenol+A+from+polyethylene+terephthalate+drinking+water+bottles+of+China

hours. And, after all your efforts, the last thing you need is to lose the dog because you passed out in the heat.

Optional Stuff

- Food Bowls (remember to clean and disinfect them before stowing)

- Hand Sanitizer

- Muzzle (in different sizes, or an adjustable one)

- Anti-Tick and -Flea Spray

- Baby Wipes (for hands, face, legs, to wipe up spills...)

- Dog Food (you might have a long wait at the vet, and you'll probably go through your make-friends bait stash quickly, so a bit of kibble might come in handy)

- Scissors and/or Knife (rescue often involves dogs tangled in fencing or brush, or with too-tight makeshift collars that will need to be removed)

Chapter 13

Letting Go

When I talk about rescue with people who have never rescued or who've had, at best, limited exposure to it, one of the things I hear most often is, "I couldn't do it. I'd want to keep all the dogs."

As if I—or any of the hundreds of rescuers out there—didn't. Dude, *all* of us want to feel that way. I've never rescued or fostered a dog that I didn't want to keep. I've cried every single time I delivered a dog to his/her new family. (Heck, I get attached even to the dogs that come in for surgery at the clinic where I volunteer.)

If you're going to be a rescuer, you need to understand this: It's About The Dog. And in a homeless dog's process of regaining quality of life, a rescuer (or foster) has a limited role. You're Mary Poppins, blown in by the East Wind when needed—and blown out when things are set aright.

Because there are other families who need her. Other situations that need 'a-righting'. From this perspective, how selfish of the Banks children to ask her to stay—and how selfish of her if she *did* stay. Tears notwithstanding (not just the children's but her own), she opens her umbrella and flies away.

Dogs are the original Zen teachers—and nowhere is this most evident than in rescue. *The origin of suffering is attachment,* says the Buddha's second noble truth. Us humans tend to equate *love* with *attachment* (which may well be the source of all evil today), but working with dogs you learn—willingly or otherwise—that love is about *letting go*.

Don't misunderstand me; this isn't about *not caring*, about hardening your heart in order to feel nothing. (You'll be an epic failure at rescuing if you do that. Remember, dogs can read you like a carnival fortune-teller.) Instead, strive to understand the temporal nature of your relationship with the dog you're rescuing (or fostering). And, maybe more importantly, the *purpose* of this relationship.

You've done the hard work; you've taken him/her off the street, you've brought him/her to safety: to the land of medical care and vaccines and people who care. If you're a foster, you've helped them heal, you've put their bodies—and their souls—back together. And yet, the most important thing you'll need to do for this dog will be allowing him/her to find the family where s/he belongs.

Every dog needs (and deserves) a family of their own. A pack—of two, of fifteen, doesn't matter; it's not about numbers but about how well the members fit together. Sometimes that pack turns out to be yours (oh, happy day!). But make sure this isn't something you're doing to avoid letting go—because that, my friend, is something you do *for yourself*.

It's About The Dog.

If you're a parent, this will sound familiar. You love your kids to bits—but would you forbid them to go to college, get married, move away and build their own lives? No. (Well, I hope not.)

Let them go. Open your umbrella and go find the next dog who needs you. There aren't many Mary Poppins in the world. Not many people can rescue, or foster. Once your job is done with this dog, you have a responsibility to the next one. (This is, incidentally, why a foster who adopts the dog they're fostering is called a *failed foster*.)

There are dogs out there waiting for you to help them. Don't let them down just because you can't let go.

Chapter 14
Medicating the Homeless

Late one morning, a (non-rescuer) friend called to say he and his girlfriend had found a dog in bad shape and they didn't know what to do. "I think he's dying," he said. "He won't move. He won't eat."

Shit.

As I drove, I prepared myself for the worst. A quick shot at the vet's, a merciful end surrounded by strangers—"but, at least, strangers who care enough not to leave you to die in the street."

I squeezed that for every drop of comfort. Didn't get even a thimbleful.

The dog was nothing but skin and bones. Mangy, watery eyes, pale gums. He panted a little (good), but otherwise didn't show interest in anything (bad). He didn't even sniff at the liverwurst I brought.

But he was friendly. He let me approach and touch him and never even flinched. I wrapped him in a big towel, picked him up and put him in the car. My friends wanted to come along to the vet, so before we drove off—and so they'd at least have the drive to process, if they decided to come after what I had to say—I gave them the speech. "You've done this dog a great, great service. We don't know how sick he is, what chances he'll have, or whether he's strong enough to fight. But I want you to know that, if worse comes to worst, you saved him from dying out here, alone, and probably in a lot of pain. That's probably more kindness than he's ever had in his life. So... Chin up. Okay?"

Their smiles were wan, but they did follow me—us—all the way to the vet.

The vet's diagnosis was grim: heartworms, tick fever, sarcoptic mange, anemia (see *Health Issues*, p. 63). This dog was an elderly chap, 8 to 10 years old, which meant both heartworms and tick fever had probably been around for years. But—and I still get choked up about this—the vet didn't think euthanasia was necessary. "He's not that far gone," she said. "He needs to gain some weight before we treat the heartworms, but he can get antibiotics for the tick fever now. That'll give him a boost, and if he starts eating then I'd say he's got a chance."

Except... we had a problem. Because of his (highly contagious) sarcoptic mange, no foster could take him in. No shelter would, either, or boarding facility. Rightly so; the first responsibility for any caregiver is to the dogs s/he already has. But the fact remained we needed a safe place for this dog, we had to give him medicine—pills and a vitamin booster—twice a day, with food, and monitor his eating and drinking, in order to treat his mange. But we couldn't find a home for him as long as he had mange. It was a Catch-22.

The vet suggested starting the mange treatment—weekly shots—right away. "Within a week or two he won't be contagious anymore," she said. "Maybe then you'll find a foster willing to take him."

Maybe. But... Until then, what?

You might have noted the switch from *I* to *we*. It happened at some point in that examining room. My friends weren't rescuers, had never done this before. But they joined in like the best of 'em: they asked questions, they fetched paper towels, learned how to hold a dog for the vet. They grimaced but didn't turn away when the needles went in, when the skin scrapings began. (Respect for steel-stomached newbies, y'all.) They even volunteered to foot the bill. And, as their rescue baptism, they got to name the dog. They chose *Carlito* (of *Carlito's Way*).

Most importantly, though, they *committed*. Because, you see, without a foster or anywhere to take Carlito, the only choice we had left was to treat him in the street. This doesn't work always, and not every treatment can be done like this; in order to recover fully, Carlito would still need a home. But, until that particular miracle happened, we'd have to pick up the slack.

We established a twice-a-day feeding routine. It took a couple of days and a bit of "research" (asking the locals at which times they saw him), but eventually Carlito settled into it like a pro. He waited for us, he learned to recognize both our cars as soon as we turned into his street, and his greeting, as his health improved, went from limping up to the car (but always with tail wagging, even at the start when he was so weak and, we later learned, in the grip of severe arthrosis), to running in mad circles and, once the car door opened, jumping up, always gently, to the driver's seat to greet us. Once a week he got a car ride to the vet for his mange shot, and he loved that. Within ninety days he went from the saddest sack of bones to a bouncing, healthy dog.

We never did find a foster for Carlito. We didn't need to. After the summer, my novice-rescuer friends moved to a new place, and took him in. And so Carlito went home.

~ * ~

It's no secret that the real challenge of rescuing is *space*. Shelters are overcrowded (and underfunded); foster homes are about as rare as purple unicorns—and also far, far beyond capacity. Too often the unthinkable happens: you find a dog desperately in need of help and—for any number of reasons—there's nowhere to take him/her.

Let me be clear. The best option is always—*always*—to take the dog off the street. They need a safe place to recover, to heal, to regain their trust in humans. Treating a dog while s/he's still on the street can only be a last recourse.

But it *is* a recourse. One more in your arsenal of hope.

Chapter 15

New Kid in the Pack

If at all possible, and especially if you have limited experience with handling multiple dogs or dogs you don't know very well, you shouldn't attempt introducing a new dog to your pack alone. Get help: from a rescue-savvy acquaintance, from a behaviorist, from a vet, or—at the very least—from a friend who's willing to get their hands dirty. The more hands, the safer you'll all be.

Because of that space challenge we talked about—overflowing shelters, not enough foster homes—rescuers all too often end up bringing a dog home. If you have no dogs, great; go ahead and skip to the next chapter. But what if, like most of us, you already have a houseful? Will they be okay with this new (temporary, or pseudo-temporary) member of the family?

You'd think a dog would be glad to have a same-species companion, wouldn't you? And, most of the time, they do—especially if they've been the sole dog in the family. Even when there are already two or three in the pack, if they're well-socialized (i.e. dogs who are used to positive interaction with other dogs) they'll often be welcoming to new additions. But let's not forget that dogs are pack animals, after all. Their instinct is to defend the existing pack, and that defense includes driving away intruders. Your challenge (should you choose to accept it) will be to get your dogs to perceive the new kid as a member of the pack—whether s/he'll be staying forever or just for the night—and to do so as quickly as possible.

Some things you *don't* want to do

- Bring the dog in for the first time at night. For some reason, nighttime increases tension levels. If at all possible, bring him/her in with daylight, and with enough hours left in the day to work through the introductions—or lock him/her up in the spare bedroom for the night and wait until the morning to present him to the family.
- Let the newcomer meet the entire pack all at once. Do it in increments. If you've identified the alpha (the dominant member) of your pack, let him/her meet the new guy first, separate—out of sight—from the others, and see how that goes. Something that's worked for me is taking my alpha for a walk outside the house, somewhere where neither dog can feel claims of proprietorship, and focus on the walk—the actual forward movement—instead of letting them interact with each other. By the end of those walks, they're usually comfortable with each other and, most importantly, my alpha has understood that this is a dog we—as a pack—are accepting of. But for this you need an extra pair of hands, someone to walk one dog while you walk the other.
- Involve food. Dogs will protect their resources, and food—especially for a newly rescued pup—is an important one. Once they've met and seem to be getting along, you can offer a small treat to everyone as a reward for good behavior (and as reinforcement that socializing is a positive thing), but even then you'll want to throw the treat, especially the newcomer's, far from the other dogs to avoid disputes.
- Keep only one of them on a leash. There's this thing called The Law of Equal Leashing (okay, I just made that up): leashing one dog while the others are loose makes the leashed dog feel at a disadvantage, which will result in stress—and unnecessary defensiveness. Either everyone is leashed, or no one is.

- "Let them sort it out themselves." Lots of people believe in this, and all I can say to them is you've been incredibly lucky.
- Leave the new kid alone with the rest of the pack. For the first few days, you need to become a hawk: watch them constantly (and when you can't be there to watch, keep the new addition separated, preferably somewhere where the others can't see him/her) and issue corrections on any behavior that indicates anxiety, discomfort, or over-excitement. (See *Body Language*, p. 24)
- Pity the dog. S/he will sense it, and take it as indication that s/he's weaker. So will your own dogs, which might potentially become a disaster scenario. On the other hand, pity makes you more likely to let him/her get away with bullying your dogs (or you) just because *poor thing, she's lived on the street all her life*. The key to harmony is to be clear—and consistent—on the kind of behavior you expect, and will allow, right from Minute One.

Remember what we said in the last chapter about a caregiver's first responsibility being to the dogs s/he already has? When a new dog doesn't seem to be fitting into the pack, the experts often advise taking him/her back (to the shelter, to the breeder, etc). But, if it's a rescue, what are you going to do? Return the dog to the street? This means that, if your dogs and the newcomer aren't getting along, and every other option has been exhausted—a foster who might be willing to make space, a kennel where you might put the dog up for the night or for a few days, a friend without dogs (and with a walled-in yard)—you'll need to figure out a way to keep both the newcomer and your dogs safe.

And an enclosure able to contain a panicky just-rescued dog doesn't get built overnight. So make sure, *before you bring the dog home*, that you're prepared. Can a section of your yard be closed off? Maybe there's a room in your house—preferably uncarpeted; makes it easier to clean up messes—where the newcomer can feel safe, but you might want to clear out anything you're especially attached to. When dogs are stressed, they tend to become weapons of mass destruction.

Chapter 16
Other Options

So... You've decided that rescuing isn't for you. That's okay. I don't blame you. But *but* you still want to help. Here's a list of ways—spanning from the creative to the simplest to the budget-friendly (and even the no-budget)—to help *you* help *them*.

Adopt

Like Nike says... Just do it. Your best friend is sitting in a cage at a shelter somewhere, waiting for you.

Remember the seniors

Everyone wants the puppies, no one wants the grizzled muzzles. But these older guys are the ones that most need your affection. (As a reward, you get to skip right over the nightmare of puppy training.)

Foster

Can't add a dog to your lifestyle permanently? Consider doing it temporarily. Plus, costs are usually covered by the shelter or rescue organization (food, medical, etc). Check with them on their foster programs.

Volunteer

No room for a dog in your life at all? How about becoming the fun aunt or uncle? Shelters and rescue organizations are always scraping the financial barrel, which means they're not just overpopulated but understaffed. Plenty for you to do: anything from bathing dogs to walking them to playing with puppies to giving medication to answering phones. And it's at your convenience, from once in a while to every day, depending on your schedule.

Donate

Every cent helps, sure, but it doesn't have to be money. Kibble, HeartGard, anti-tick and -flea protection, shampoo, old towels and/or bedsheets, toys, treats, leashes, collars, food bowls, cat litter and litter boxes—even office supplies. Pretty much anything you can think of will make a difference. If you're a crafter, consider creating some cool donation boxes, or you can knit a gorgeous dog bed or, from old rope, make a climber toy for the kitty cage.

Let your imagination run wild. The possibilities are endless.

Sponsor

Pledge to cover the costs of a dog's upkeep. In kill shelters, dogs have a certain period from the time they're rescued or brought in to be adopted, go to a foster, or find a pledge; if none of these things happen, the place has no choice but to put them down. (And my heart breaks for the employees—and the vets who have to do this ugly, ugly work.)

Non-kill shelters and sanctuaries need sponsors, too: they're committed to keeping the dogs they receive for as long as it takes for them to find a home—and if no home is found, the dog will live out his/her life there. But, with the adoption/rescue ratio being so disproportionate, their population is at a constant increase, and resources must be divvied up among more and more mouths. For these organizations, being able to count on your regular support (or even sporadic, if you can't commit monthly or yearly) means they're able to guarantee proper medical and preventive care for their residents—and they can rescue one more dog.

Medical sponsor

Let your vet know you're willing to help out a dog owner who can't afford a necessary treatment for their dog. Be as general or specific as you like: maybe you want to sponsor a sterilization surgery, or the first batch of vaccines for a litter of puppies. Maybe you want to keep it on a case by case basis. It's up to you. (If you don't have a house vet, check with local shelters for some suggestions.)

Become a home-finder

Marketing professionals, this is you. Help your local shelter or rescue organization promote the animals ready for adoption. This can be as easy as talking to your friends about it (and asking them to talk to *their* friends), or designing flyers, or talking to a local magazine or newspaper about running a (free) ad featuring a weekly dog, or... Any other cool ideas?

Put your unique skills to work

If you're an accountant, volunteer to help out with the shelter's admin. If you're a graphic artist, maybe you can design some cool posters to promote adoption or raise funds. If you're in PR, help them organize their next fundraiser. If you're a lawyer, you could volunteer to help with legal issues, or get involved in lobbying for animal-friendly legislation. If you're in construction, volunteer as a handyman once a month. If you're a social media maven, maybe you can help run their Facebook and Twitter pages. If you're a writer, you could write copy for them: leaflets, flyers, ads, their website. Whatever you're good at, I guarantee it can save lives.

Avoid pet shops that sell puppies

This may be the most important contribution of all. Even if you're just buying fish food, or a leash for your niece's stuffed poodle, please buy it from a store that doesn't sell puppies (or any animal, in fact). Commercial breeding is the largest single factor responsible for the dog overpopulation problem we have today, and darn hard to put a stop to—because it's good business. As long as breeders are able to sell all their puppies, they will keep on breeding. And, let's face it, responsible breeders—the kind who care for the parents, who monitor the mom's health carefully for the full three years before she's allowed to breed, who carry out strict checks on the people who want to buy the puppies, or who only sell to people they know and know well—these breeders aren't the ones whose puppies end up in pet stores. No, pet stores largely get their 'inventory' from backyard breeders, from people out to make a buck who give not a single iota for the dogs themselves. (And, if you ever saw the mother, the conditions she's living in, and to which she's condemned *for life*, you'd be more likely to take an ax to the store owner rather than bring them your business.)

Over the last decade (and, here in Curaçao, over the last two or three years), the non-puppy-selling pet store has become more and more visible. There's one close to you, I bet. Look for it. Forgo convenience for conscience. It's worth it.

Chapter 17

The Rescuer's Pack

No rescuer is an island. If you're going to make this rescue gig a success, you're going to need help. And I don't mean just the occasional goodwill of a random passerby. No, you're going to need support you can count on, from people who care—about you, sure, but also (mostly) about the dog—and who know what they're doing.

In other words, you're going to need *a pack*.

Vet Team

What's the first thing you do when you (finally) have your fresh-from-the-street rescue in the car? *You go to the vet.*

Which one, though? If you're a brand-new rescuer, you might not have a 'bedside' vet, and you might be tempted to stop at the first Veterinary Clinic sign you see—which is still better than going straight home. But, if you're going to jump head-first into rescuing, you'll need a vet you trust. One who keeps careful, methodic medical histories. One who's familiar with the health issues associated with living in the street—and in your particular area. (For example, vets who move to Curaçao from abroad, especially from first-world countries where stray dog populations are under control, have seldom—if ever—seen tick fever cases as severe as the ones we commonly find on the island's streets.)

You also want a vet who will give it to you straight; in rescue, sweetening the pill doesn't help anyone, least of all the dog. And one who'll be willing to consult with a colleague (or three) when an issue stumps him/her. (Which is why many rescue organizations work with a veterinary team rather than a single individual.)

Fellow Rescuers

There is nothing more frustrating than trying to catch a dog, especially a skittish or fearful one, on your own. Sometimes you'll be part of a rescue team, but sometimes it'll be just you—and for those times it'd be oh-so-nice if you had a friend or two on speed-dial you can count on to help you. They don't need to be experienced rescuers; they don't even need to like dogs (but it helps, mostly for their sake). They just need to *be there*. Maybe hand you a leash, or play Bad Cop to your Good Cop in a chase.

One of the hardest parts of rescue is the tough decisions. The life-or-death calls. As discussed in *Euthanasia* (p. 48), these are decisions that you shouldn't have to make alone. You'll need the vet's perspective, certainly (and most importantly), but you'll also want to have the input of a rescuer friend (or three), if only for perspective.

Behaviorist

No one is as full of creative and out-of-the-box ideas than a dog behaviorist. (They're the ones that inspired that "Out of the box? What box?" thing.) And when it comes to difficult rescues, nothing beats having a behaviorist's resourceful thinking on your side. Careful with abusing this privilege, though. Pick up the phone only when you *really* need to.

Beyond the actual rescue, a behaviorist is essential to assess the dog's state of mind and offer a prognosis on putting their soul back together. Love is good—it's key, in fact—but there are wounds that might require specific healing. A behaviorist will be your go-to resource for those.

One Eternal Optimist

At *least* one. Rescue takes a lot out of you, emotionally, so you'll want to have someone on hand that keeps your spirits up, someone who's always willing to Look On The Bright Side of Life.

Chapter 18
Q & A on Rescue

We adopted our dog from the shelter. Does that make us rescuers?

It makes you heroes. The *crème de la crème* of humanity. The redemption for the sins of uncountable thousands. The example, the exception, the light. (But... No. Not rescuers.)

I'm currently fostering a dog for a rescue organization. That makes me a rescuer, right?

It makes you a *foster*, which is beyond essential to rescuing. Put simply, there could be no rescuing without fosters. All these dogs we pick up off the street—in terrible shape, with diseases or wounds that will take time to treat and heal, and with broken souls—need a place to go and someone to put them back together, mind and body, before they can go on to a forever home.

But, unless you were involved in the actual street chase, diving under cars and all, you're not a rescuer. Fostering is separate from rescuing—and comes with its own challenges (and, as you've probably found out by now, its own joys).

I picked up a puppy wandering in a supermarket parking lot and brought him home. That definitely makes me a rescuer. (Right?)

Kudos for the initiative, but... No. (*Sigh.*) Here's why:

- Are you sure it was a stray? Could it maybe have been just lost?
- Street-born puppies rarely wander off by themselves. If he really was a stray, chances are he had siblings somewhere

close by. (And a mom.) You might have missed a good chance of getting a whole family off the street.

- Did you take him straight to the vet? Yes, before taking him home. A clean bill of health is essential to prevent the spread of infectious diseases or skin conditions. Plus, he'll need his first vaccinations.
- Are you prepared to keep him? Do you have the budget (for food, medical care, behavior training), the time, and the space? If not, do you have a network you can connect with to find him a good foster or forever home?

I want to help, but all that sounds too complicated. Isn't something better than nothing?

Something is, indisputably, better than nothing. *But it needs to be the <u>right</u> something.* (Think of it this way: you don't call an electrician to fix a backed-up toilet.)

If you're serious about wanting to help, get in touch with your local shelter and/or rescue organization and ask them who you can call when you spot a possibly stray or lost dog. Ask them also about their volunteer programs. You can give a (much needed, and much welcomed) helping hand at your convenience, and at your time, budget, and experience capabilities.

Rescue is much too difficult; I could never do it.

Actually, rescuing is pretty simple. It's time consuming, and it's an emotional roller coaster, and it can be very, very frustrating... But the mechanics are simple. In terms of qualifications, what you need is:

a) A deep love and respect for any form of non-human life;

b) Humility (you'll need to ask for a lot of help, from a lot of people; you'll also very, very often make the wrong decisions and screw everything up);

c) An open mind.

I'd love to get involved with rescuing, but I'm not allowed to keep pets where I live now.

Many people confuse *rescuing* with *fostering*. Rescue is the act of catching a street dog and taking him to safety; fostering is providing that safety. Lines blur; rescuers end up fostering, fosters go out on rescue missions. But the fact remains: you can be a rescuer without fostering, and you can foster without rescuing. *And* you can help immensely without doing either. Check out *Other Options* (p. 98) for a list of cool ideas; you can do tons without even leaving your living room couch. And you can always contact your local shelter or rescue organization. They always need an extra pair of hands.

Why are there so many more women than men involved in rescuing?

Like most preconceived notions about rescue, this one's part myth and part truth. Plenty of men are involved in rescue—and they're darn good at it. But—and this is a fact—dogs tend to find female humans less scary than male humans. Maybe it's the voice (higher vs. lower pitch). Maybe it's the perceived dominance of a male scent. Maybe it's hormones. I don't know. So men who rescue are at a slight disadvantage. Slight, I say, because it's nothing that can't be overcome by the right approach.

I tried to adopt from a rescue organization but the whole process took weeks, and was totally bureaucratic. Why all the questions? Why all the hassle?

Remember when we said It's About The Dog? That means It's Not About You. Rescue organizations—and, increasingly, shelters as well—focus on the dog's needs and do their best to find them not just a home but a family. People who will care for and love him/her for as long as the dog lives.

Some of the concerns when matching a dog to a home:

- Does the home have space enough to accommodate the dog's needs?
- Is the home and/or yard fenced in properly? (Remember, most long-time strays and ferals have a Houdini gene.)
- Does the dog's primary caregiver have enough time to meet the dog's exercise needs?
- If there are other pets in the home, will they accept the newcomer? Does the family have enough experience—or is willing to get help—to deal with the introduction and with the adjustment period?
- If there are children in the home, or children frequently visit the home, is the dog a suitable match for them? What ages are they? Are their parents experienced dog owners who will provide guidance and supervise interaction?
- If the dog hasn't been spayed/neutered yet (the case of puppies, for instance), can the family guarantee s/he will be sterilized as soon as the surgery is viable?
- Can the family afford proper medical care for the dog?
- What is the likelihood that the family will make a major move (say, overseas) in the near future? And, in the event of such a move, are they prepared to bring the dog along?

None of these things can be determined through an application form or a fifteen-minute chat. It takes time (and at least one home visit) to get a picture of the life a dog will have with them. Not every family, or every environment, is suited to every dog. And a dog that's already been through so much deserves every advantage we can give them.

If you're interested in learning more, many rescue organizations include on their websites a sample questionnaire for potential adopters, their adoption policies, and even a breakdown of their screening process. A simple online search should give you a list long enough to keep you busy the whole afternoon.

Why do shelters charge an adoption fee? I mean, if it's a homeless dog and I'm taking it off their hands, shouldn't it be (at least) free?

Seriously? If this is the way you think, you shouldn't own a dog. Any dog.

(Fine. I'll play nice.)

Shelters aren't running a business. They're not turning a profit, or distributing dividends to their shareholders. In fact, adoption fees are so low they barely cover the basic medical expenses (vaccines, monthly anti-tick and -flea prevention tablets, sterilization)—and they certainly don't even make a dent in the enormous amount of resources—money, time, effort—the shelter/rescue has put into this particular dog. No, the main reason for an adoption fee is to make sure you're serious about adopting. In this currency-oriented world we live in, there's a neuron somewhere that fires a message whenever we have to pay for something, saying, This here is worth it. Because you paid for it.

And, also, if you can't afford the adoption fee—$75-$150 on average, in the US[11]—you certainly can't afford the (much steeper) medical care the dog will need during his/her life.

So there. Go home. *Without a dog.*

Which brings me, rather pointedly, to the next question...

Why are rescuers so unfriendly, so intolerant, so... RUDE?

We're not, actually. Not to animals, anyway :) I wouldn't appreciate someone else putting words in my mouth, so I'll speak for myself and myself only here. Have you ever noticed how a shelter's or rescue's PR person is rarely, if ever, involved in the actual rescuing? Nothing strange about it; you wouldn't ask a hospital's accountant to go fill in at the ER—and I'd love the spectacle of a surgeon trying to balance the accounts.

---

[11] http://www.dogsonly.org/adoption_fee.html

Everyone has their job, everyone has their passion... And, for a rescuer, it's—you guessed it—ABOUT THE DOG. So, when I witness human cruelty and neglect (as in actually see it happening) every day, it's probably not difficult to understand that humanity doesn't score high in my book. And, when I see people around me, people whom I've had serious conversations with about the evils of breeding, go and buy a Rottweiler puppy (OMG, the parents won a competition in Wherevershire last year!), it shouldn't be hard to understand why I'd rather choke them than say hello to them.

In short: I'm not a people person. I'm a dog person. And an animal person. (And yes, I realize I'm rude and obnoxious to non-animal persons. And I'm sorry for it. Sort of.)

I get why commercial breeders are bad. But what about hobby breeders, people who only breed a small number of litters a year and carefully screen adoptive families, as opposed to the mass-breeders at animal mills?

For me, this is a case of choosing the lesser evil. Small, caring breeders are certainly better than puppy mills that keep dogs in unspeakable conditions—but they're still evil. Well, not evil, but... you know. Not good.

Why? Let me explain.

First, the whole breed thing smacks of racism to me. Would you choose your friends based on their skin color, their place of birth, where their parents come from? (If you would, then you're reading the wrong book.[12]) Are these things relevant to this person's character? Maybe. But having a Mexican best friend in fifth grade doesn't mean you'll even like other Mexicans. And if your "Mexican" friend turns out to be 50% Peruvian, does that automatically make her more—or less—likeable?

---

[12] May I suggest a copy of *Mein Kampf*, perhaps?

Second, breeding is a hard, hard thing to do responsibly. The mother's health needs careful monitoring; she can only give birth limited times (not once a year), and only after she's 2 years old. She can't be force-bred in any way. And any breeding with which humans interfere becomes an anti-natural-selection process, which perpetuates faulty genes (witness, for one example, the German Shepherd propensity for hip dysplasia).

Third, the reason we have homeless dogs to begin with is because there are too many dogs. And not enough homes. So, until a good, healthy chunk of the world's homeless animals get a home, I can't condone any breeding at all.

I realize the large majority of the world doesn't feel this way. All I can say is, if you absolutely cannot live without a pedigreed whatever-breed in your home, please—please—look at shelters and rescue organizations before going to a breeder. Any breeder. A full quarter of the dogs in shelters are purebreds. There are even rescue organizations devoted to specific breeds (the American Kennel Club[13] publishes a list every November).

If you're considering adding a dog to your family, please— please, *please!*—give a home to a dog who's already here, instead of aiding and abetting yet another litter of puppies to come into the world.

---

[13] http://www.akc.org/dog-breeds/rescue-network/

Chapter 19
Right & Wrong

In rescue, *right* and *wrong* are rather ephemeral concepts. Too many variables involved. Every situation is different. Every rescuer is different. And every *dog* is different. All of which make it annoyingly difficult to find a fail-safe, cookie-cutter, A-B-C rescue formula.

There are thousands of rescue videos out there. Zillions of websites on dog behavior. Hundreds of books on animal health and psychology. And hordes of experts—real experts, impeccable credentials, success after success in their résumés—with diametrically opposite views.

Dogs are like wolves; no, dogs are *very different* from wolves.

Dogs need to know you're the alpha male; no, dogs need to trust you.

Dogs can be vicious; no, dogs only attack when provoked.

You should approach a dog from above, to show him who's boss; no, you always approach from below, to gain their trust.

The list goes on, and on, and on.

Life isn't easy for a newbie rescuer. With all these opposing views, how do you know what's right and what's wrong? How do you separate the wheat from the chaff? And, more relevantly to the dog who's waiting out there for you to get your crap together and come save the day, how do you decide on an approach?

- **Do your own research.** Nothing beats finding out stuff for yourself. Check every fact. Even when you agree with someone's point of view, make a point of reading up on the opposite side. This isn't about being right (or wrong). It's About The Dog.

- **Treat the dog like an individual.** No two dogs are alike. Even brothers who grew up together and have been exposed (and not exposed) to the same experiences, who've received the same training, who have the same humans and receive the same level of love and attention, will develop different personalities—and different responses, especially to stress. So you can imagine how much more different street dogs will be, not just from a family dog but from each other. The experiences they've gone through, the close calls they've had, their genes... It's all a big unknown to us as rescuers, but it all plays a part, and your biggest mistake is to ignore that. No dog is *just a dog.*

- **Try, try again. And again. And again.** Trial and error is the way of rescue. I cannot begin to tell you how rare it is for a rescue attempt to succeed on the first try. (And even if *you* succeed on your first try with that dog, remember there's probably been at least one more person who tried and failed.) What sets rescuers apart from kind souls who would help if they could (meaning *if the dog came knocking on their door*) is perseverance. The dogs that most need help are the ones least likely to just let you catch them—so it's those that most deserve your efforts. Over and over.

- **Consensus breeds confidence.** Remember that *Pack* we talked about (p. 102)? The group of people you're supposed to collect to help you in your rescuing endeavors? Consult with them. Get their ideas, mine their experience, pick their brains. If you can get agreement from at least two of those trustworthy few in your corner, you know you've got a winner plan.

- **Go with your gut.** There's no overestimating the power of your own instinct. What *feels* right to you? What are your other, not-so-obvious senses telling you? These will be the things that are hardest to communicate to a non-observer— but they'll often be the ones that make the biggest difference.

If you're a rescuer, you know that beginner's luck may be rare but it *does* happen (to the frustration of the experienced rescuer who has failed where a newbie succeeds). The truth, though, has less to do with luck and much, much more to do with mindset.

I don't mean in any *think positive* or *visualize your success* sort of way. Here, I'm talking logic and approach. The newbie, being a newbie, has no previous experience to bring to the rescue— which has all sorts of drawbacks, sure, but may give them an edge: an open mind.

Once you've been rescuing for a while, it's easy to forget that dogs, like people, are individuals. It's easy to start lumping them together, prejudging, assuming. And, when you start taking things for granted, you start missing opportunities. You get into a rut, a routine, and you stop thinking outside the box.

When a newbie succeeds at rescuing a dog who's been eluding you for weeks, instead of fuming and muttering about *beginner's luck*, feel grateful. You've just been given a reminder to step out of your box.

Chapter 20
Sterilization

What do we dog people mean when we say *sterilization*? We use the term rather loosely, and mostly we actually mean spaying or neutering, but *sterilization* actually encompasses a broad gamut of procedures, from surgical to non-surgical, and with varying degrees of both effectiveness and permanence. Researchers are still exploring possibilities, especially in the non-surgical field. Not all of them are practicable, or recommendable, on rescue dogs, but you can find tons of information on these if you're interested. Here's a brief overview to get your toes wet:

Non-Surgical Sterilization
Chemical castration
A solution (preparations and products vary, but the most common are calcium chloride and zinc gluconate) is injected directly into the testicles, which kills the tissue and causes sterility. If done properly, may have permanent results.

Pros:
• Non-surgical, which means less risk of sedation-related pulmonary and/or cardiovascular complications.
• Recovery time is faster than surgery.
• No stitches to remove.
• No wounds, thus a presumed low risk of infection.

Cons:
• To achieve effective sterilization, the solution needs to be injected not just at the right spot but also at the right *depth*

inside the testicle. The vet doing the injecting is essentially working blind, and there is no reliable way to tell if it's been done right. In a field trial in Mexico, several dogs developed ulcers at the injection site. In the Galapagos Islands, some developed necrotizing reactions at the place the solution was injected. In most cases, repairing the damage of botched chemical castration requires more extensive surgery than repairing surgical castration complications.

- Most vets agree that sedation is probably necessary anyway, if only to ensure the dog stays still for the injection. The genitals are not an area where you can afford to have faulty aim, after all. And the effectiveness of the injection relies on accuracy.

- Pain. Very little information is available on how much pain the procedure causes the dog, not just at the time of injection, but also as the testicular tissue dies.

- Prognosis. Even if sterilization is successful, there is not enough research on the effects the dead testicular tissue will have on the dog's overall health in the long term.

- Because there is no change in the appearance or size of treated testicles, it will be impossible to identify an animal as sterilized. This makes it necessary to have permanent ID measures in place, either via chipping or tattoos.

Contraception

Hormones and Immunocontraception

Dogs receive hormones, either via an implant or orally, that regulate fertility: production of testosterone and sperm in males, of estrogen and eggs (*ovum*, if you want to get all technical) in females, or a vaccine which produces antibodies that shut down the production of reproductive hormones.

Pros:

- Non-surgical, which means less risk of sedation-related pulmonary and/or cardiovascular complications.
- Recovery time is faster than surgery.
- No stitches to remove.
- No wounds, thus very low risk of infection.

Cons:

- Physiological risks and side effects can be serious (just like with humans) and require careful monitoring. One of the most life-threatening for the 'injectable pill' in dogs is bone marrow suppression, which can be permanent and result in death.
- Because hormonal cycles vary, it's very difficult to tell the exact date to start dosage.
- Duration of sterilizing effect may also vary, which makes this a method of low reliability.
- Implants must be renewed and oral medication must be provided (and made sure it's ingested), which requires easy access to the female. In stray dog or wild animal populations, this is impractical and demands a dedicated staff.

Surgical Sterilization

Fallopian tube ligation (females) or Vasectomy (males)

Just like in humans, this procedure involves tying off the conduits of eggs (fine, *ovum* then) and sperm to avoid reproduction.

Pros:

- Effective and reliable method of birth control.
- No pills, implants, injections.

<u>Cons:</u>

- Comes with the same risks of any surgery: potential infections at the incision site, potential complications from sedation, stitches.
- Compared to a spay or neuter surgery, ligation or vasectomy procedures tend to take longer, thus increasing anesthesia-related risks as well as surgical complications.
- Although it may be functional as a means of preventing reproduction, it lacks the guarantee—and the life-saving physiological benefits—of removing the ovaries or testicles, and therefore also the added benefit of hormonal influence on behavior.

Spay (for females) or Neuter (for males)

In females, the removal of the ovaries (and uterus, as recommended by the surgeon); in males, the removal of the testes.

<u>Pros:</u>

- Sterilization is permanent and non-reversible, making this the safest birth control method.
- Removal of the ovaries and testes results in significant physiological benefits to the dog's health:
  - ✓ risk of ovarian / testicular cancer reduced to zero;
  - ✓ a non-spayed female has seven times the risk of developing breast cancer compared to a spayed female (especially if spaying occurs before her first heat);
  - ✓ risk of other cancers linked to hormones (such as anal gland and prostate cancers) also reduced markedly;
  - ✓ notably less risk of contracting TVTs (transmissible venereal tumors);
  - ✓ behavioral issues related to hormones diminish dramatically if not disappear altogether, especially when

spay/neuter occurs on or before 6 months of age. For instance, intact males will mark their territories (read piss all over your house) much more than neutered ones. And, in a multi-dog household, hormones are the original apple of discord. If all your dogs are spayed and/or neutered when young, conflicts defuse faster and escalate slower.

✓ in males, the diminishing of the instinct to chase a female in heat, instinct which results in escapes, accidents, getting lost, fighting, and the potential to contract all sorts of disease and parasites.

Cons:

• Comes with the same risks of any surgery: potential infections at the incision site, potential complications from sedation, stitches.

Oh, I know. It's such a harsh word, isn't it? Sterilization. *Sterile.* Makes one think of moonscapes, cold and barren. Of merciless sun on endless dunes. Of desolation. Despair.

And yet, when it comes to dogs, *sterilization* is how we spell *hope.*

An estimated *three-quarters* of the world's dogs are unwanted. Homeless, surrendered to shelters, abandoned, living in the streets. An overwhelming majority won't get a happy ending; there simply aren't enough homes.

And most of these dogs are fertile. Which means they're reproducing. The problem isn't getting better, it's getting *worse.* Non-surgical options aren't practical; they're too expensive, too unreliable, too experimental. As much as we do, as many dogs as we rescue, as many as may somehow find loving homes, there will never be a real solution to the problem of overpopulation and homelessness will never get better without a widespread practice of systemic sterilization.

But why should you, a responsible owner, have to spay or neuter your dog? (I mean, *puppies!*) Plus, *you* would never abandon your dog. Your dog will never know a homeless life.

Think about this for a second. Can you really—absolutely, without any caveat of any kind—guarantee that your dog will never end up in the street? What if s/he gets lost? What if s/he's stolen? Oh, and don't forget Mother Nature. Storms, earthquakes, fires—they shatter more than just human lives. Hurricane Katrina, for instance, left over 250,000 animals homeless. That's *a quarter of a million.* Hurricane Harvey left at least 2,000 pets homeless—and this was the count at the beginning of September 2017, just after the disaster hit.

None of these animals' owners were prepared for this. (If they had been, they would've chipped them. And they would have *spayed* or *neutered* them.)

Chapter 21

The Trust Quadrant

Throughout this book, we've been throwing around the word *trust* like a pinball. Getting the dog to trust you is, after all, the cornerstone of rescue. So maybe it's time to talk about what *trust* means to a dog—and how you go about getting into their good, trusting, graces.

Dogs are, by nature (and by human domestication) not leaders but followers. They don't want the Alpha role—and they'll take it on only when they feel they have no choice. Which is often the case on the street: through abandonment or abuse, a street dog's covenant with humanity has been broken, and so they've had to rely on themselves to survive. But, at the core of every dog, is a nugget of instinct and desire to find safety—and that safety comes in the form of a pack, and a strong leader.

That means you.

Humans, being the clueless idiots we are, tend to equate leadership with loudness, strong personality, even violence. Dogs, being so much more intelligent than us, see this for the bullying it is—and the weakness it exhibits. For a dog to sense you as a leader, you'll need to show four things:

Balance. You can't be nervous. You can't be excited. You can't be angry, or sad, or frustrated. Okay, let me rephrase: you *can* be any of these things, but *you can't let them control you.* If you're not in control of your emotions, how could you ever be in control of the pack? Get in touch with your Zen. Breathe.

Assertion. Being assertive isn't dominance. It's not a "my way or the highway" thing; your way *is* the highway—to safety, to a happy ending for the dog. Believe it, and the dog will believe it, too.

Respect. Don't just look at the dog; *see* him/her. Observe their attitude, their body language. Seek to understand them, and—more importantly—their needs. Establish a line of communication, but not of the *here boy* kind; your body speaks volumes, much louder, and more effective than any words. Avoid looking them straight in the eye; dogs read eye contact as aggression. Don't move so fast; give them time to get used to you, to read you, to understand what you want. Bring your hands in from below, never from above. Always keep whatever you're offering—food, your hand, a leash—under their nose. (Remember *Botched!*, p. 29?) Use your body language to make it clear you understand what they're saying to you (*I'm afraid, I don't know what you want*), that you respect that, and that you have something important of your own to say (*I'm here to help. You don't have to be alone anymore*).

Honesty. Dogs can read you better than a fortune teller at a county fair. Dogs sense ulterior motives, so honesty really is your best policy. Keep your bag of tricks, such as traps, for the very last of recourses—and, when you do use those, brace yourself: you'll have a hell of a time gaining that dog's trust afterwards.

Balance, assertion, respect, and honesty.
The Trust Quadrant.

Chapter 22

Universality

Compassion is an action word with no boundaries.
~ Prince

Dog rescuing comes with consequences. A houseful of dogs, for instance. An ever-growing dent in the balance of your bank account. A fast-track education in veterinary medicine—and on the basics of Zen philosophy. Some of these consequences you might expect, many you probably don't. Like how you'll start judging others by their attitude toward dogs. Or how your priorities will shift... All of a sudden those *when I win the lottery* dreams become less about yachts and round-the-world trips and more about buying a piece of land and turning it into a dog sanctuary.

Most of all, though, you'll begin to notice a broadening of your perception. A certain *universality*.

Rescue, at its core, isn't about a love of dogs. That might well be what brought you to it, but, once you're in it, you'll realize there's a weird alchemy at work in your soul. Rescue, you see, is about compassion. And compassion is universal.

Compassion doesn't restrict itself to a certain breed or a certain size or even a certain species. Compassion for one is compassion for all. It will happen before you know it; maybe your vet will raise an eyebrow the first time you show up with a pigeon or lizard or hamster, but by the time you start coming in (or calling them out to the middle of nowhere) with a horse, a goat, a deer, a... well, whatever form of life needs your help (and theirs), they'll know to expect you with the broad-spectrum vet kit.

The thing is, not every vet can deal with any animal, or any emergency. And your local dog shelter will probably balk at housing a raccoon with a broken leg. So here's my advice to you, dear Rescue Padawan. Do some research on the wildlife in your area. Are there any species that, like raccoons or possums, might be considered pests? Those are the most likely to cross your path in need of rescue. There might even be organizations devoted to their protection and welfare; many offer brief training or information sessions, even online.

Your focus might well remain on dogs (or cats, or whatever started you rescuing), but consider this your fair warning: even if it does, your attention span *will* widen to include other species. Prepare yourself.

Chapter 23

Vets, Unsung Heroes

So you think rescuers have it bad? Putting their lives on the line with strange, scared dogs capable of anything? Yeah, it's a rough life. But you know who else does that? *Every* day?

Vets.

In fact, vets may well be the most undervalued of animal welfare heroes. They do so much, and get so little recognition.

Being a vet is kind of like a mash-up of all the negative aspects of being a doctor (for humans), without any of the pluses. Think about it. Veterinary med school is just as hard, takes just as long—but with one crucial difference: you can count on one hand the ones who'll ever come close to making the big bucks people doctors make. Their patients can't talk, can't say where it hurts or what they last ate. At least pediatricians have a parent to fill in the blanks—and a mom or dad can usually be trusted to follow instructions, call if something looks or feels wrong. (You wouldn't believe how many dog owners don't.) Also, people doctors restrict them-selves to either general medicine (for anything more than the common cold they'll give you a referral) or a particular specialty—and only for a single species (humans). But vets are expected to cover *all* the specialties, from reproductive health to ophthalmology to X-ray technician to microbial and bacterial diagnostics to odontology—even surgery! *And* they're expected to do all that not just for dogs and cats but for *all sorts of species*.

Try asking your ophthalmologist about your digestive problems. Try asking him about your *dog's* digestive problems.

No, being a vet isn't easy. And, as if all of the above weren't enough to qualify them for *most challenging profession ever*, they get all sorts of crap over their fees. You've no idea how often I hear people—*smart* people—complain about the vet bills they have to pay. Not long ago, in the vet's waiting area, I witnessed a woman who refused to pay her bill. She'd brought in a puppy who had been diagnosed with parvovirus, too advanced to do anything but give him a painless way out. But his owner, this woman, didn't want to pay for the euthanasia. "Why do I have to pay? He's going to die anyway, right?"

She preferred, rather than pay a measly 50 bucks, to take the puppy home and let him die on his own, in pain.

(The vets waived the fee—which is to say, they paid for the injection themselves—and put the puppy down anyway. The woman left happy.)

This is why, back when I was around 15, I decided against becoming a vet. This situation, with me as the medical professional, would've ended in a lawsuit. Or me in jail. And this is, too, why vets are my heroes. The idiocy they put up with, the costs they absorb, the strength of character and the patience they exhibit to educate the more-often-than-not clueless, and only sometimes well-intentioned people who walk through their doors...

And then there's the actual patients. A vet's physical integrity is on the line with every single patient they see, Chihuahua dog or Arabian stallion. We rescuers talk about building trust and taking our time, we talk about kits and traps and tranquilizers, and then we celebrate when, after three weeks, we finally get a dog into a car. The vet? S/he won't get any time to *make friends*, or *earn the dog's trust*. S/he's got a job to do—and that job means putting fingers and even noses closer to those unfriendly and very strong canine jaws than any rescuer. Do they balk? Do they say, *Well, maybe we can try tomorrow?*

No. They GET THE JOB DONE.

Oh, and then there's the rescuers themselves. "But this is a *street* dog. You should be doing it for *free*."

Look. Vets volunteer enough of their lives to animal welfare already. They've committed *their entire careers* to low wages and the hardest, broadest, most challenging of medical professions *because they care*. No one becomes a vet for the money, or for glory, or even for academic recognition. No one's going to win a Nobel for veterinary medicine.[14] No one's going to name a hospital after you. No, if you chose to become a vet, it's because your desire to help animals trumped every other consideration.

Compared to vets, then, us rescuers are nothing but dilettantes.

Seriously. Hug your vet today. Bring them some coffee next time you visit. Some homemade cookies. And, please, don't complain about your vet bill. If you have reason to believe you're being overcharged—I won't deny it happens; there are unscrupulous people everywhere—then change vets (because, if their ethics are faulty that way, then your dog isn't in safe hands anyway). But do your research. And check *why* a certain vet might be more expensive than another. If it's talent, or commitment, I suggest you pay up.

---

[14] Dr. Peter C. Doherty, awarded a Nobel prize in 1996 together with Rolf Zinkernagel (MD), for their discovery in the early '70s of how T cells recognize virus-infected cells by looking for variants in certain molecules on the surface of infected cells, was a state veterinary officer in Australia before embarking on a career in immunology research. https://www.avma.org/News/JAVMANews/Pages/111201o.aspx

Chapter 24

Who Rescues Who?

Rescued by a rescue dog! Like something straight off a bumper sticker. (Cue the pink heart-shaped paw prints.) Sounds suspiciously similar to the born-again raves of people who've found religion, doesn't it? Right up there with 'God is my copilot' or 'Jesus loves you (but I'm his favorite)'. And you—a rational, unsentimental, mature human being—can't help but snort: *Oh, puh-leez.*

Oh, ye of little faith.

The dogs we rescue—and the act of rescuing itself—come with rather unexpected windfalls.

Your Own Strength

Rescue will break your heart: the abuse you'll witness, the sheer helplessness, the dogs you can't save. The pain will take you by surprise the first time. It hurts so much, so deep, you feel you must die of it. So you swear you'll never do it again. But then there's the next dog, and—how can you say no? How can you not *try*? So you do it again—and again, and again—and at some point you realize that, although a heart broken for the 1,000th time hurts just as bad as the first, it's still not enough to kill you. Not even close. Somewhere along the way you've come to understand that the pain you feel is the only love that dog likely ever knew, and so straighten your shoulders and dig for hidden reserves of strength to bear it with honor.

Resilience

The stray dog's superpower. When we humans get sick, when life gets hard in any way, we tend to fall into self-pity. *Why is this happening? Why me?* We wallow. We give up. We let whatever happened to us take over not just our present but our future.

I guarantee whatever that was doesn't even come close to the misery that is the life of a stray dog: day after day, minute by minute, a litany of terror and uncertainty, of pain and hunger, of illness and lovelessness. Never-ending. And all of it through no fault of their own. For no reason at all (except the ignorance, most of it willful, of humankind), the destiny they face is the bleakest: dying alone, most probably in pain, most depressingly unloved.

And they don't give up. Give them a quarter or even an eighth of a chance—a little medicine, a little love, a little food, a little time—and they're more than ready to move forward and leave the past behind. Where it belongs.

Scratch a stray dog and find not just an unbending will to survive but an indomitable *joie de vivre* that puts all our human drama to shame.

Perspective

Because rescue exposes you to all sorts of horrid things, you learn pretty fast to focus on the good stuff. Your newfound strength helps you cope with the bad stuff, and the resilience you witness helps you find the silver linings: there is always a glimmer of light, a reason to be grateful. The smallest step forward—even the absence of steps backward—become glorious triumphs. And, eventually, this perspective begins to leak into your personal life.

Selflessness

Compassion is a key component of the path to illumination in many religions: Christian charity, the *rahmah* of Islam, the *rahamanut* of Judaism. It is the foundation on which the entirety of Hindu philosophy stands on. The Buddha teaches it is only through compassion and wisdom that enlightenment can be achieved.

Why? These religions don't agree on much, but they all do agree on the importance of compassion. Is it just because *being kind* guarantees good social order? Is it the tribute that whatever god or gods you believe in demand as a sort of ticket into paradise? Or is it something else, something deeper?

I believe so. After all, an act of compassion done in order to achieve a reward in the afterlife—that's to say, done for our own benefit—can hardly qualify as compassion at all, right? Kindness extended to a stranger in the hopes (or even in expectancy) of the favor being returned in the future, or at the very least of some gratitude, isn't really kindness at all, is it? In human interaction, however, that's pretty much what happens.

But with animals the mechanics change drastically. A dog can't return the favor, can't even feel gratitude in our human sense of the concept—and even if they could, they can't express it in the uncertain terms we talkative bipeds most appreciate (more on this in *The Gratitude Myth*, p. 57). As the owner of a rescue dog, you might disagree—but, remember, the rescuer's role is a different one. Whoever rescued that dog is, most likely, long gone from the dog's life. They can't see how far the dog has come, how much weight s/he's gained, how his/her behavior has improved by leaps and bounds. They don't get to see the tail wags or the licks or the looks that you interpret as 'gratitude'. Which means the rescuer did what they did without expecting any of it. Selflessly.

And that is the core of compassion. Acts of absolute selflessness. That's why religions put such high importance on it: compassion is the gateway to selflessness, which leads to empathy, which leads to a sense of genuine communion with everything around us. And it's that communion what constitutes illumination.

Forget the pearly gates, or karma, or 72 virgins. In fact, forget any religious doctrine, any spiritual belief. You want to be 'saved'? Come save a dog today. Rescue is the one thing in the world that's absolutely guaranteed—I'm talking 100%-money-back pledge here—to make you a better human being.

Chapter 25

The X Factor

So what is it, once all is said and done, that makes the difference between a successful rescue and a failed one? We've been talking about what to do and how to do it, but—really, does this all add up to a fail-safe recipe for success in dog rescuing?

Short answer: No. (Wow. Shortest chapter in the book.)

Of course, it's not that simple. There are too many variables in dog rescue. Too many unknowns. Too many X factors.

Beginning with the dog, of whose history you know nothing. You may assume and deduce and guess, but... no, not *know*. Same goes for his/her character. And these two things, their history and their character, are a huge factor. How skittish is s/he? How responsive to the lure of food? Plenty of strays and ferals prefer the safety of distance to the reward of even the tastiest morsel.

The location also plays its role: is the dog in a trash dump, in an abandoned lot, is the area close to a busy intersection? Any of those will require a different rescue approach. The clothes or shoes you're wearing, the equipment you may (or may not) have in your car, the time of day, the people you're with (or without)...

Regardless of the integrity of your intentions and your own preparation and experience, any number of things over which you have absolutely no control have the potential to affect the result.

It can be something as idiotic as your phone ringing just as the dog is beginning to come closer. Or a curious stranger approaches and scares them off. Or workmen nearby choose that moment to start up their hydraulic drill. It can be something as unforeseeable as the dog having negative associations to the food you're using as bait.

But, sometimes, these variables play right into the plan. Sometimes everything just falls into place. Sometimes what seemed like a disaster ends up being a most unexpected windfall. Maybe the dog, given the choice between hydraulic drill and scary human (you), will decide you're the lesser of the evils and run into your arms. Maybe your scent is similar to someone's that the dog loved once, and your fellow rescuers will watch on in amazement as this frightened, catch-me-if-you-can dog approaches you with ears down and tail wagging, and begs for a belly rub. (Remember that bit about beginner's luck in *Right & Wrong*, p. 112?)

When stuff like this happens, you realize that your role in this whole thing is actually very, very small. Rescue truly is about being the right person at the right place at the right time. And that *rightness*... well, it just can't be predicted. As I said before (*Right & Wrong*, p. 112), rescuers differ from other animal lovers in that they're willing to put in the effort—the chase, the weeks of building a feeding routine, the counter-intuition of approaching a snarling dog to slip a leash around his/her neck— to find out. And willing, also, when the *rightness* simply isn't there, to try again. And again. Over and over.

The difference between a successful rescue and a failed one? Nothing less than *blind, cosmic luck*. You can get the odds to lean in your favor if you're prepared, if you have some experience, if you're in the right mindset. But, bottom line, what will make you a successful rescuer is perseverance. *Stubbornness.* When everything fails, you don't give up.

Because you have the absolute certainty that, sooner or later, that X factor will be in your favor. And you have the patience to wait for it.

Chapter 26
Youth vs. Age

What are the pros and cons of rescuing older vs. younger dogs? Is it really easier to rescue a puppy than a senior?

Puppies *can* be easier. They tend to follow Mom's example, and if Mom is approachable, chances are the puppies will be, too. Even if she isn't, though, if the puppies are young enough (under 12 weeks), their natural curiosity might still work in your favor. A good rescuer can take advantage of it, and turn the whole rescue into a game.

In a puppy, also, the natural affinity dogs have for humans might still be unchecked by negative experiences (which produce fear), so although they might be wary at first (they've never seen one of us), the domestication gene may be a good rescue ally.

But—you knew there was a *but* coming, didn't you?—not all is peaches and cream with those cuddly balls of fur (i.e. they're not always quite as willing to be cuddled as we'd like). Some of those fear-producing negative experiences seem to be passed on genetically. We fostered a dog once who turned out to be pregnant, probably had just become so a couple of days before we picked her up, and although her puppies were born at home and never knew a bad experience (trust me, we kept three of them—one of them, in fact, is Sam, the dog on the cover of this book—and they've been as spoiled as any dog ever could be), they're still fearful.

If Mom isn't around, and especially if the puppies are under 8 weeks, their instinct is to hide... Which makes them incredibly hard to find. (Remember *Botched!*, p. 29?) Also, they rarely come singly—there's usually a litter—so you're going to have to deal with several of them at once. Pick carefully which one you'll get first; if that intrepid explorer gets spooked, cries out or fights you as you pick him/her up, chances are the rest of the litter will run and—yep, hide.

And you also have the mom to contend with. Even the most docile of dogs will become a lioness when her babies are in (what they perceive as) danger.

Adult dogs, on the other hand, may *seem* like a tougher job for rescue—but they don't have to be. If they've survived on their own for however long, it means they're street-smart, which may mean they'll be warier of humans, but may also mean they have the necessary experience to make judgment calls: is this a *good* human, or a *bad* human?

Don't misunderstand me; these judgment calls don't happen overnight, certainly not in a few minutes. What I mean is that these dogs will be willing to give you the chance—they'll stay at a safe distance, and watch you from there—to show your true colors. But that is one chance, and *one* chance only. Squander it at your own, and the dog's, peril.

Because of these street-smarts, adult dogs may also fall easier into a feeding routine than puppies, and, through it, into a relationship with you. Adult dog brains (just like adult human brains) are already wired to look for the pattern, to understand cause and effect, to analyze possible outcomes. If you are constant and consistent, if you follow *The Trust Quadrant* (p. 121), you have a good chance of establishing yourself in their good graces.

~ * ~

The truth is that, like with everything else concerning rescuing, the issue of age cannot be taken as hard and fast. The only rule, when it comes to dog rescue, is that every dog is an individual. Every situation is unique.

As they're so fond of saying in investment disclaimers, *past behavior is no indication of future results.* No truer words...

Chapter 27

Zealots

Animal rescue, like anything that involves intense emotional involvement—religion, politics, vaccines—has its share of zealots. *I am the sole possessor of Truth. Righteousness is mine.* (You know the type.)

Look, I have nothing against deep convictions, or the passion to defend them. But there's a fine, and murky, line between that and bigotry.

You'd think rescuers, being so compassionate, would extend at least some of that compassion to fellow humans, even to the ones who aren't quite *there* yet in terms of illumination, those whose understanding of the stuff that really matters, is somewhat under-developed.

Alas, no.

You want to make an enemy for life? Piss off a rescuer.

Granted, we probably won't get pissed at any of the 'normal' stuff, like you standing us up for a date, or posting an unflattering photo of us on Facebook; it'll be over the fact that *You bought a puppy WHERE???* Or because you moved and, instead of bringing your dog along, you rehomed him. Or maybe you happened to mention in passing that you're looking for a purebred male to mate your pedigreed Afghan hound.

Whatever it is, chances are you won't understand what you did wrong. But the consequences will be swift. *And thus the red right hand of god smote the heathen heretic in holy righteousness.*

I am not free of sin, so this isn't about throwing stones—or, rather, if any stones need to be thrown, this is me volunteering as target practice. The truth is that it's this zealous attitude of rescuers that gives all of us, even—maybe especially—large-scale organizations like PETA and Greenpeace, a bad name.

If rescue is about improving the quality of life for animals, those of us involved in making it happen *need to rethink our strategy*. I don't mean that we all need to become fake-smiley PR-ey lobbyists, but... Maybe just tone down the bigotry. Just a tad.

It is, after all, About The Dog.

(And, one of these days, I'll start listening to my own advice.)

Afterword
Sasha's Story

Remember Tiny Dog, from *Catch Me If You Can* (p. 34) and *Drugs* (p. 42)? Maybe you're interested in how her story ended. As you might remember, the restaurant people who wanted to adopt her backed out in the end, and understandably so. They really wanted a dog to cuddle and play with, and she was never going to be that dog. So she stayed on with us.

At first we did intend to find a home for her, once she became more sociable, maybe less of a flight risk, but... well, she never did. Not enough, anyway. She did learn to trust us, somewhat, but she was terrified of any other human. Five years after her rescue she still remained a shy dog who rarely came when called (unless you were the bearer of goodies such as, say, leverworst or—her personal favorite—roast beef). In the evenings, though, when we were watching TV, she might sidle up to the sofa and peek up at us with those cute brown-black eyes of hers to ask for an ear rub and a chest scratch. We always obliged, as long as she was doing the asking. Otherwise, we chose to give her space. We wanted her to understand we were prepared to wait, that we expected nothing, that she could come out of her shell when (and if) she felt comfortable doing so. Other than for vet visits, when we had to corner her to get a leash on and carry her into the car, into the vet's office (she really, really hated leashes), we refused to force the issue.

Perhaps we should have.

She got along with our other dogs (except for one, but I'll get to that). She developed a certain closeness, you might even call it a friendship, with two; we witnessed actual playful moments between them every now and then. With the rest it was mostly interactions of the live-and-let-live sort, but we were content with that. Often, in a multiple-rescue-dog household, that's the healthiest outcome one can hope for.

It wasn't all sugar n' spice, though. Early on, one of our dogs—Benny, brother to Sam and part of the litter of puppies born here at home just six weeks after Sasha came to live with us—seemed to develop a particular dislike for Sasha. Maybe it had to do with the fact that, when we were weaning these puppies by soaking dry food in milk, Sasha used to nudge them out of the way and steal a bit of food if we weren't watching. Maybe Benny never forgot that (although the other puppies seemed to; one even became one of the dogs Sasha grew closest to). Maybe Sasha's fear triggered something in Benny. Maybe the lipoma (tumorous growth of fatty cells) she developed on her right hind leg exuded an odor offensive to Benny. Maybe it was its shape—being inoperable, it grew huge. Maybe it made him perceive her as weak, a hazard to the pack. Maybe, as one behaviorist friend suggested, he never even acknowledged her as 'dog', never recognized her as belonging to the pack at all, but instead—because of her size, or shape, or behavior, or lipoma, or all of the above—saw her as prey.

And he attacked.

It happened, at first, over food. Predictably. So we made a point of keeping them somewhat separated at mealtime. But then it began happening over—well, nothing. Nothing that I could see, anyway. Most of the time they were fine around each other. And then, out of the blue, Benny attacked.

Now, I'm fine with a dog establishing boundaries. If another dog comes too close, or plays too rough, or disrupts the hierarchy, a growl or a snap, what we call a 'warning' bite (meaning a bite not intended to do actual harm), is absolutely called for—and is actually an important part of achieving harmony in a multi-dog household. Dogs are much better 'listeners' than humans, so these warnings need happen but once, maybe twice, and the lesson is learned.

But that's not what Benny was doing.

He drew blood. More often than not, his attacks ended at the vet. Blood was spilled. Stitches required. Granted, these incidents only happened once, maybe twice, a year. Which was a mixed blessing: obviously we didn't want Sasha to get hurt at all, but if these attacks had happened more often, perhaps it would've been easier to spot the causes, the triggers, and therefore deal with them. Because so much time passed between incidents, we were lulled into complacency, into believing whatever we'd done—separate them for meals, scold Benny, pay more/less attention to one or both of them, reinforce the hierarchy, etc—had solved the problem.

And then it would happen again.

This past year things escalated. We saw three attacks in as many months, and each one got worse. Because of the size and location of her lipoma, the wounds more often than not were on it, which made it difficult for them to heal. Time and again, the vets that stitched her up warned me that she might not make it—but she was more resilient than any dog her size has a right to be, and she kept surprising us all.

The last incident happened when we weren't home; with no one to interfere, the attack went too far. We came home to find the front porch splattered with blood, and Sasha's hind leg—the one with the lipoma—torn open. We rushed her to the vet, and amid much head-shaking and general caveats on how this time it really might not heal, they managed to patch her up as best they could. She was put on antibiotics, and strict twice-a-day topical treatments to help the wounds close.

She died in the early hours of July 26th, 2017, ten days after the attack. She died in pain, unfortunately, but with my hand on her head and chest to, I hope, soothe her somewhat. To let her know she was loved, even if I hadn't been able to do right by her.

Of course I could have saved her. She and Benny should never have been left together without supervision. Maybe they should never have had to share a home, even. I should have put more effort into finding her a family of her own, somewhere without other dogs or with dogs her size, dogs who accepted her. I should have understood that Benny's aversion to her wasn't temporary, that it was connected to a trigger deep in his psyche. He didn't attack her out of malice; Benny is a sweet, sweet dog, himself fearful, and so eager to please. He attacked her because he felt it necessary to do so. Could he have overcome that? Maybe. But he was never going to do it on his own. *I* was the one responsible for spotting it, identifying it as a serious problem, and developing the training routine necessary to help him. To help them both.

Sasha died long before her time. She was around six years old; by all rights, she should have lived at least five more years, maybe even ten. That she didn't is my fault. I'm not punishing myself over this; I'm not looking for absolution or sympathy. What I *do* want is to learn from this. Learn, so that I may never again put one of my dogs at risk—especially not in their own home. I believe that every dog should have the inalienable right to feel their home is a safe haven; that is why I rescue. But in Sasha's case—and, somehow, in Benny's, too—I failed.

I will not fail again.

Perhaps Sasha's death is too recent for me to have already processed all the lessons I need to learn from her—from her life, and from the end of it. But one thing is clear to me, even in the midst of the grief: the solution isn't, and never will be, to give up rescuing. Yes, we make mistakes. Yes, we screw up horribly. Yes, it's impossible to forgive ourselves. And, yes, perhaps we would indeed be better off *not* rescuing; we wouldn't have to put our hearts and souls through the wringer. But...

Well. You already know what I'm going to say. It was never about my heart, or my soul. It was never about *my* anything. In the world of rescue, *it's about the dog*. The existing dog, the one who needs me to become a better carer, in order to keep him/her safe. The *next* dog, the one still on the street, the one who needs me to become a better rescuer, in order to give him/her a chance at a life worth living.

Perhaps most of all it's also about the dog I let down. Wouldn't giving up be the ultimate betrayal? If Sasha paid with her life for my mistakes, shouldn't I honor her by making sure she didn't die in vain?

It's the very least I can do.

Acknowledgments

The fact that this book came into being is an act of absolute serendipity. Never would have happened without the blogger community encouraging me to write the original blog post series, or without their wonderful support through an entire month of posts—including many comments and questions that not just helped make the book version stronger but also started enlightening conversations. I'm looking at you, Jeffrey—Michelle—Debbie—Roland—Damyanti—Susan—Ann! And at the DoggieCaperz blogger (whose name I don't know) for the suggestion of including an eternal optimist in the rescue pack (*The Rescuer's Pack*, p. 102). Thank you.

I would have had nothing to write about, however, if I hadn't come across—and been taken in so warmly by, despite my lack of experience (and lack of Dutch and Papiamentu)—the dedicated rescue organizations of Curaçao. The Curaçao Animal Rights Foundation (CARF), for instance, which was not just my entry into the island's world of rescue but my window into an entirely different, much deeper understanding of rescue itself. Stichting Dierenhulp, a foundation dedicated to providing free sterilization surgeries for pets whose owners cannot afford to pay: volunteering with them I achieved a lifelong dream of not just observing but even assisting the surgeons inside the operating room, and I learned incredible amounts. Feed Friends, the angels in SUVs and hatchbacks who drive around the island feeding the street dogs that shelters don't have place for: they're the last line of defense, and so many dogs out there owe them their lives.

The world of rescue is a lonely one; not many 'normal' people understand a rescuer's priorities or preoccupations, or why we devote so much time to something that makes us, 90% of the time, so miserable. Which is why having other rescuers around is so important. And I've been blessed with the best of them. Mirjan Seppenwoolde, Djoeke Giliam, Miriam Oria, Dyveke Fraaij-Brugman, Sheila Maal, Karin Wooning, Lida Molenaar, Babette de Waele, Lydia Vroegop, and the many others with whom I've shared rescue adventures—thank you so, so much. All the right stuff about rescue that I know, I learned from you.

An essential part of rescue is behavior, and I've been fortunate in getting to work—and getting to know—the best behaviorists on the island. Esther Platell, who sadly has since moved away from Curaçao (but is building a successful practice in her new home in Germany), was elemental in introducing me to the joys and challenges of understanding canine behavior. She mentored me with saintly patience even though I knew nothing—no, let me amend that: I did know some things, but they were all *wrong*. Esther washed out the myths and prejudiced tenets from my brain and basically reeducated me from scratch. Thank you, Esther. It's too bad all our work didn't get Nassau the home (and happiness) she deserved, but all those lessons learned from both you and her will stay with me for the rest of my life.

Eveline Reints, from the island-wide famous Yuka's Honden-training, took over where Esther left off. I have, quite literally, become a better person for training at her field—and so have my dogs. If Esther taught me the theory, it's been with Eveline that I've put it into practice, and this has helped me become a better rescuer, too.

Els van den Eshof, Eveline's partner-in-crime, and a superb consultant for complex behavioral issues, has saved my meager butt more than once—and improved my canine family's life exponentially. Without Els and her observations of my pack, my understanding of the angst and fear (and their expression) in dogs I rescue would be far, far more limited.

I owe an enormous debt of gratitude to the veterinarians at Veterinary Centers Curaçao, who have not only put the bulk of their professionalism, their combined expertise, and their compassion at the service of countless rescued dogs and cats (and their often hapless rescuers—yes, I speak for myself), often going above and beyond the call of duty to help, to accommodate the weird schedules rescue demands, to donate their time and skills to rescue organizations, but have also somehow found the time to answer my endless questions, to patiently explain complex procedures and fill in my very basic gaps of scientific understanding. Dr. Quenny Dols, for instance, agreed to take me on as a surgical assistant during my 28 months with Stichting Dierenhulp, trained me, taught me, and even, totally selflessly, offered to read the sections in this book that referred to veterinary medicine in order to give me invaluable feedback (and caught many stray misnomers and misused terminology; thank you, Quenny). I am rather stubborn, though, so any mistaken or incomplete information is solely my own responsibility.

Boundless gratitude as well to the friends who eagerly volunteered to read this manuscript to help with formatting (Connie Golsteijn, you aced it!) and to provide author blurbs. (Robin and Lynne, you're superstars, and your feedback was invaluable.)

Finally, there would be no *A-to-Z Guide for Wannabe Dog Rescuers* at all if publisher extraordinaire Matt Potter (of Pure Slush Books and Truth Serum Press, as well as this imprint) hadn't taken the time to read that original blog post series and seen some sort of potential in them, enough to turn them into a book. Matt, your patience and dedication have been *sine qua non* in shaping this project. Thank you, everlastingly, for believing in it. (And for being such a wonderful dog parent.)

I'd be remiss in closing this Acknowledgments section without mentioning you, Reader. I think, if you made it this far, you must care deeply about dogs' welfare, and—on behalf of all rescuers, here in Curaçao and around the world—I can never thank you enough for that. I hope these pages have been useful in helping you understand the world of rescue. And I wish you much success with your first rescue. Go get 'em! They've been waiting for you.

About the Author

Guilie Castillo Oriard is a Mexican writer and dog rescuer living in Curaçao. She misses Mexican food and Mexican *amabilidad*, but the laissez-faire attitude (and the beaches) are fair exchange. And the bounty of cultural diversity provides great fodder for her obsession with culture clashes.

Guilie's work has appeared online and in print, and she blogs at http://guilie-castillo-oriard.blogspot.com. Her novella *The Miracle of Small Things* was published by Truth Serum Press in 2015.

It's About the Dog is her first non-fiction book. Follow Guilie's dog blog at http://lifeindogs.blogspot.com.

Also from EVERYTIME PRESS and TRUTH SERUM PRESS

https://everytimepress.com/everytime-press-catalogue/

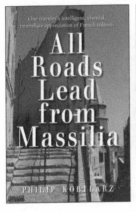

- *All Roads Lead from Massilia* by Philip Kobylarz
  978-1-925536-27-0 (paperback) 978-1-925536-28-7 (eBook)
- *Lenin's Asylum* by A. A. Weiss
  978-1-925536-50-8 (paperback) 978-1-925536-51-5 (eBook)
- *Inklings* by Irene Buckler
  978-1-925536-41-6 (paperback) 978-1-925536-42-3 (eBook)

- *all you need is … a whiteboard, a marker and this book*
  by Matt Potter
  978-1-925536-27-0 (Book 1) 78-1-925536-28-7 (Book 2)
- *Kiss Kiss* by Paul Beckman
  978-1-925536-21-8 (paperback) 978-1-925536-22-5 (eBook)